T0361233

ROUTLEDGE LIBRARY EDITIONS:
URBAN STUDIES

Volume 21

RACE AND GENDER DISCRIMINATION ACROSS URBAN LABOR MARKETS

RACE AND GENDER DISCRIMINATION ACROSS URBAN LABOR MARKETS

SUSANNE SCHMITZ

Routledge
Taylor & Francis Group

LONDON AND NEW YORK

First published in 1996 by Garland Publishing, Inc.

This edition first published in 2018
by Routledge
2 Park Square, Milton Park, Abingdon, Oxon OX14 4RN

and by Routledge
711 Third Avenue, New York, NY 10017

Routledge is an imprint of the Taylor & Francis Group, an informa business

British Library Cataloguing in Publication Data
A catalogue record for this book is available from the British Library

ISBN: 978-1-138-89482-2 (Set)
ISBN: 978-1-315-09987-3 (Set) (ebk)
ISBN: 978-1-138-03695-6 (Volume 21) (hbk)
ISBN: 978-1-315-17816-5 (Volume 21) (ebk)

Publisher's Note
The publisher has gone to great lengths to ensure the quality of this reprint but points out that some imperfections in the original copies may be apparent.

Disclaimer
The publisher has made every effort to trace copyright holders and would welcome correspondence from those they have been unable to trace.

RACE AND GENDER DISCRIMINATION ACROSS URBAN LABOR MARKETS

SUSANNE SCHMITZ

GARLAND PUBLISHING, INC.
NEW YORK & LONDON / 1996

Library of Congress Cataloging-in-Publication Data

Schmitz, Susanne.
  Race and gender discrimination across urban labor markets /
Susanne Schmitz.
       p.   cm. — (Garland studies in the history of American
labor)
  Includes bibliographical references and index.
  ISBN 0-8153-2392-1 (alk. paper)
  1. Discrimination in employment—United States. 2. Sex
discrimination in employment—United States. I. Title. II. Series.
HD4903.5.U58S32 1996
331.13'3'0973—dc20
                                                   96-17462

Printed on acid-free, 250-year-life paper
Manufactured in the United States of America

For Hannah and Adam

Contents

List of Tables

Acknowledgments

I am indebted to many individuals for their help and support in completing this project. I wish to thank John Garen, Frank Scott, and Nancy Johnson of the University of Kentucky for their constructive comments on earlier versions of this work. I am especially grateful to professors Mark Berger of the University of Kentucky and James Marsden of the University of Connecticut for their guidance and support throughout the various stages of this project.

I have benefitted significantly from the supportive atmosphere provided by my colleagues and the administration at Elmhurst College.

I also wish to thank Sue Callahan for typing the first version of this manuscript, and the editorial staff at Garland Publishing for their patience and assistance.

Special thanks go to Paul E. Gabriel of Loyola University Chicago for his helpful comments and tireless editorial assistance.

Although this project would not have been possible without the assistance of these individuals, I accept complete responsibility for any errors or deficiencies which remain.

Race and Gender Discrimination Across Urban Labor Markets

I

Introduction

Economic discrimination is said to exist in a labor market when two groups of workers, who have the same abilities, education, training and experience, are accorded differential treatment with respect to hiring, occupational access, promotion or wages. Groups of workers may be discriminated against on the basis of characteristics that might include (but are not limited to) race, age, sex, religion, or national origin. Since the 1960's, the federal government has passed an array of antibias laws and regulations (e.g., The Equal Pay Act of 1963, the Civil Rights Act of 1964 among others) designed to prohibit many forms of labor market discrimination in the United States. Since that time economic research has proliferated in the area of labor market discrimination. Much of this research has investigated the existence of economic discrimination against groups such as women (Blau and Beller 1988; Blau 1984; Beller 1985 among others) and minorities (see Carlson and Swartz 1988; Reimers 1983; Gwartney and Long 1979 as a few examples).

This study investigates the effects that local labor market conditions may have on the economic status of women and blacks, relative to their white male counterparts. More precisely, it examines the impact that local labor market conditions have on estimates of labor market discrimination against women and blacks. The two forms of labor market discrimination investigated in this study are: (1) wage discrimination — paying equally productive workers different wages on the basis of considerations not related to productivity, and (2) occupational discrimination — assigning workers to different jobs on the basis of nonproductivity related factors. The notion of labor market discrimination used throughout this book is that taken from Arrow (1973) where "personal characteristics of the worker unrelated to productivity are . . . valued in the market" p. 3).

While it is our intent to examine what effects local labor market conditions have upon the relative economic status of women and blacks, we also intend to specify an appropriate definition of a local labor market. Many studies examining discrimination make use of a national labor market (see Blau and Beller 1988; Carlson and Swartz 1988, Albelda 1986 as a few examples). However, at any given time, one can observe wide variations in labor market characteristics (such as unemployment rates, industrial composition and employment, labor force participation patterns, to name a few) across smaller geographic labor markets. In October 1980, for example, unemployment rates at the state level ranged from a low of 3.8 percent in Nebraska to a high of 12.1 percent in Michigan (Census 1981). Within these states, unemployment varied even further at the metropolitan area level. During this same period (October 1980), unemployment in Nebraska ranged from a level of 3.3 percent in Lincoln to 5.3 percent in Omaha; while in Michigan, unemployment ranged from a level of 8.0 percent in Ann Arbor to 16.3 percent in Detroit. The heterogeneity across localities of unemployment rates (or other characteristics) may or may not be an indication of distinct local labor markets. If policy makers focus their attention on an aggregate figure, such as the national unemployment rate, as a measure of labor market performance, they may overlook the effects that local unemployment rates (and other characteristics) have on the relative earnings and occupational position of women and minorities.

The organization of this study is as follows: Chapter II summarizes important works from the discrimination literature and discusses empirical techniques for analyzing wage differentials among two groups of workers. Chapter III outlines possible reasons why certain forms of discrimination, if present, may be exacerbated by certain local labor market conditions. Chapter III also outlines empirical models that are later employed to determine the extent of wage and occupational discrimination against women and blacks. We also assess the potential effects of local labor market conditions on estimates of race and gender discrimination. Chapter IV presents the empirical specification and results of the wage models while Chapter V presents the specification and results of the occupational models. Chapter VI summarizes the findings and presents possible avenues for further research.

II

Review of the Literature

INTRODUCTION

Extensive research has been conducted in the area of labor market discrimination and the advancements that minorities such as blacks and women have made in today's labor market. Economic research tends to focus on the relative economic status of these groups (see Blau and Beller 1988; Freeman 1981; Reimers 1983; Smith 1984; Blinder 1973; Oaxaca 1973; O'Neill 1985; Shulman 1984, 1987, O'Neill and Polacheck 1993; Saunders 1995; Gabriel, Williams, and Schmitz 1990 as a few examples) and how well these groups have fared since the federal anti-discrimination legislation of the 1960's (see for example Albelda 1986; Freeman 1973; Brown 1982; Beller 1979, 1982; Heckman and Payner 1989; Leonard 1984a, 1984b).

The federal government passed an array of programs in the 1960's to address labor market inequities such as discrimination. One of the first pieces of legislation to deal with wage discrimination by sex was The Equal Pay Act of 1963, an amendment to the Fair Labor Standards Act. The major provision of the act was to make it illegal for employers to pay men and women different wages for "equal work on jobs the performance of which requires equal skill, effort, and responsibility, and which are performed under similar working conditions" (Equal Employment Opportunity Commission 1981, p. 34). The act thus mandated that men and women receive "equal pay for equal work" but mentioned nothing about hiring or promotions (i.e., other possible forms of labor market discrimination).

Another major piece of anti-discrimination legislation is the Civil Rights Act of 1964. Title VII of this act makes it illegal for an employer

> to fail or refuse or hire or to discharge any individual, or otherwise to discriminate against any individual with respect to his compensation, terms, conditions, or privileges of employment, because of such individual's race, color, religion, sex or national origin (Equal Employment Opportunity Commission 1981, p. 4).

The act, as amended in 1972, applies to employers with 15 or more employees who are in an industry affecting interstate commerce, employment agencies, labor unions with membership of 15 or more individuals, and state and local governments. To enforce the act, the Equal Employment Opportunity Commission (EEOC) was established. Initially, the EEOC was limited to investigations and mediation of complaints brought to its attention, but since the 1972 amendment, it has the authority to initiate and bring suit against employers who are in violation of the law.

Other policies aimed at eliminating inequalities in the workplace are Executive Orders issued in 1965 and 1967. In particular, Executive Order 11246 of 1965, regulates federal contractors and subcontractors. The order prohibits discrimination on the basis of race, gender, color, religion, or national origin, and in certain situations, requires affirmative action programs to better the employment opportunities for women and minorities (for a discussion of affirmative action programs and requirements see Twomey 1990, pp. 83–87).

While the research on the impact of such legislation is voluminous, conclusions reached by economists remain in dispute. For example, Richard Freeman (1973, 1981) argues that a decline in the black/white wage gap, coupled with the upward occupational mobility of blacks leads to optimistic inferences concerning the decline in racial discrimination and success of federal anti-discrimination legislation. Butler and Heckman (1977) question this conclusion as they cite other reasons for the narrowing of the black/white gap. They argue that the expansion of welfare programs decreased work incentives which, in turn, led to low-wage, low-productivity blacks dropping out of the labor force. The median wage of blacks would, thus, increase, resulting in an increase in relative black/white earnings. Butler and Heckman claim that there is little evidence to support the notion that as a group, blacks have benefited from the anti-discrimination legislation. Shulman (1984a; 1984b; 1987) contends that Freeman and others take into account only some of the components of labor market discrimination. Shulman notes that while wages and occupational positions between the races may be converging, unemployment and employment rates continue to diverge. Thus, he concludes that economists such as Freeman may be erroneous in their optimistic conclusions concerning the fall in labor market discrimination — especially in light of the deteriorating relative economic position of black men during the 1980's (Saunders 1995, Darity and Myers 1993).

More recent works exploring the impact of Title VII and affirmative action programs include those by Heckman and Payner (1989), Leonard (1984a, 1984b); Smith and Welch (1984, 1989); Beller (1982); Brown (1984). In general, these works contend that federal programs have a positive impact on the relative economic status of minorities and women. Gunderson (1989) warns, however, that with respect to women, "data problems and difficulties in disentangling the pure legislative effect from the myriad of other factors that have changed in the labor market for females over the same period suggests that these estimates should be used with caution" (pp. 63–64). Similar caution with respect to estimates for minorities has been stated by Brown (1984) and Smith and Welch (1989).

WAGE DISCRIMINATION

Four primary approaches to the economics of discrimination are: (1) neoclassical theory with an emphasis on the human capital paradigm (see Becker 1971; Arrow 1972, 1973; Blinder 1973; Oaxaca 1973a, 1973b; Chiplin and Sloane 1976a; Butler 1982); (2) statistical discrimination (see Aigner and Cian 1977); (3) segmented labor market analysis, which is also known as the dual labor market hypothesis (see Doeringer and Piore 1971; Reich, Gordon and Edwards 1973); and (4) Marxist analysis (see Franklin and Resnik 1974: Reich 1977). Although the latter two are proposed as alternatives to neoclassical theory, neither has received as extensive theoretical and empirical work as the neoclassical approach (see Marshall 1974; Cain 1976). Statistical discrimination is the result of imperfect information, where employers base their decisions on information that is thought to be correlated with productivity, e.g., education, experience, etc. By basing their decisions on average measurable characteristics of a group, employers may give systematic preference to one group over another. Although employer decisions are not motivated by prejudice, the results of this model have the same appearance as the neoclassical model (see Ehrenberg and Smith 1994, p. 423). Given the preeminence of theoretical and empirical work in neoclassical economics, we adopt the neoclassical approach for analyzing wage discrimination in this text.

The seminal works of Becker (1971) and Arrow (1972, 1973) are accepted as the comprehensive neoclassical contributions to the study of racial (and gender) wage discrimination (Marshall 1974, p. 1112–1113; Blau 1984, p. 22). The Becker-Arrow framework assumes that "some economic agent has some negative valuation" on associating with certain labor groups (Arrow 1973, p. 6). The possible discriminating agents are the employer (who is willing to sacrifice profits to reduce or eliminate the avoided group) or employees (who might be willing to accept a lower wage so as to avoid working with the shunned group).[1] In these cases, the economic agents have a "taste for discrimination."[2]

Employer discrimination. In keeping with the Becker-Arrow analysis, we impose the following assumptions: (1) there are two groups of workers, A and B, which are perfect substitutes in production;[3] (2) there are a large number of firms producing a homogeneous product with identical production techniques; and (3) there is a taste for discrimination by some employers against workers from group B (Arrow 1973, pp. 6–7; Joll et al. 1983, pp. 131–135).

Consider the case of a single employer with a taste for discrimination. The firm seeks to maximize utility (and not profits) which depends upon the level of profits (π), as well as the number of B workers employed (Arrow 1973, pp. 6–11; Becker 1971, pp. 39–50; Joll et al. 1983, pp. 132–137). The utility function can be given by:

(2-1) $U = U(\pi, B)$

where $U_\pi = \dfrac{dU}{d\pi} > 0$; $U_B = \dfrac{dU}{dB} < 0$; $U_{BB} > 0$.

Assume the firm is operating in a competitive market, facing a product price P, and output level Q. Holding capital constant in the short run and given A and B are perfect substitutes, the production function becomes (ignoring capital):

(2-2) $Q = A(L) = Q(A+B)$

where L represents the firm's labor force (that is A + B). Profits are then:

(2-3) $\pi = P^{*}Q(A+B) - w_A A - w_B B$

where w_A and w_B are the wages for A and B respectively. Substituting equation (2–3) into equation (2–1), the utility function becomes:

(2-4) $U = U[P^*Q(A+B) - w_A A - w_B B, B]$.

Taking the partial derivative of equation (2-4) with respect to both A and B results in:

(2-5) $\delta U/\delta A = U_\pi (P^*Q' - w_A)$ and

(2-6) $\delta U/\delta B = U_\pi(P^*Q' - w_B) + U_B$

where Q' is the marginal product of labor (MP). To maximize utility both (2–5) and (2–6) must be equal to zero, so that:

(2–7) $P^*Q' = w_A$ and

(2–8) $P^*Q' = w_B - U_B/U_\pi$

If the firm is a profit maximizer, the profit maximizing rule is that the firm will hire workers up to the point where the marginal revenue product of labor (MRP = P^*MP) equals the wage. This is shown in equation (2–7) for workers from group A. Expression (2–8) shows that the firm will hire B workers up to the level at which its MRP equals $w_B - U_B/U_\pi$. The term $(-U_B/U_\pi)$ represents what is commonly called the discrimination coefficient (d_B), or $d_B = -U_B/U_\pi$. This coefficient "is the negative of the marginal rate of substitution of profits for B labor" (Arrow 1973, p.   7).   Given the assumption $U_B < 0$, the firm practicing discrimination will have a positive discrimination coefficient. Thus, the employer acts as though B workers cost more than their wage (Becker 1971, pp. 16–17).

Given the employer's taste for discrimination,

(2–9) $W_A = W_B + d_B$

such that the wage for A laborers exceeds that for B ($w_A > w_B$) in order for the employer to hire both types of labor.[4] With convex indifference curves most employers will employ both A and B workers. Corner solutions, however, are possible under certain circumstances (e.g., linear indifference curves; or if $w_A = w_B$, firms will hire only A workers; see Arrow 1973, for a discussion).

The market wage differential between w_A and w_B is determined by total demand for workers and the supply of B workers. Different firms will have different values for the discrimination coefficient, d_B, given their differing tastes for discrimination against workers from group B. If there are more B workers than nondiscriminating firms (whose value for d_B equals zero), those unemployed B workers would seek employment with discriminating firms who have positive values for d_B. Discriminating firms will hire B workers only if there is a differential between w_A and w_B (see equation 2–9). Workers from group B will continue to seek jobs with discriminating firms until a market wage differential is established (Becker 1971; Arrow 1973). As Arrow states, "General equilibrium requires full employment of both [types of] workers; the wages of both will adjust to clear the market, and discriminatory tastes will be reflected in wage differences." (Arrow 1973, p. 6). This implies that workers from group A earn a higher wage than those from group B, although the two groups are assumed equally productive.

Wage Discrimination in the Long Run. The usual competitive firm's profit maximizing decision rule is to hire labor up to the point where the wage rate equals the marginal revenue product of labor. Firms then establish a queue of applicants based on the expected productivity of the workers. For any given wage then, firms will hire and promote those workers who possess the highest marginal products. The discriminating firm, however, will hire and promote workers based on nonproductive distinctions and will, thus, pass over more productive workers of the nonpreferred group (B) to hire those individuals whom the firm prefers (A) (Shulman 1987, p. 364; 1984 p. 116).

If the discriminating firm is committed to attracting the preferred A workers, it may encounter the following difficulties. First, the firm could be employing less productive A workers at the given wage (this would assume that there are different types of A workers). Second, in order to attract qualified A workers, firms will have to offer higher wages, especially if the market establishes a wage premium for group A (see the previous section). Third, it may face longer search time in finding qualified workers from group A. Thus, by practicing discrimination the firm is faced with higher costs. Nondiscriminating firms will hire more type B workers and face lower costs, and hence higher profits. Higher profits should induce discriminating firms to employ more B workers or go out of business. As more B workers are employed (via the competitive process) the wages of workers in groups A and B will converge and wage discrimination should disappear in the long run (Becker 1971; Arrow 1973; Blau 1984; Shulman 1987).

Given the apparent persistence of discrimination over time, additional analyses have developed to explain this. One explanation, offered by Becker (1971), is that discrimination may persist if the discriminating firm is operating in a noncompetitive industry (pp. 46–47). Becker hypothesized that on average, employer discrimination should be less in competitive industries than in monopolistic ones. There is considerable debate, however, regarding the effect of market structure on wage differentials and discrimination (see for example Johnson 1978; Long and Link 1983; Hendricks 1977; Shackett and Trapani 1987).[5]

Another explanation is offered by Madden (1973). Madden makes use of Robinson's monopsony model to explain wage differentials by sex. The approach here is that a discriminating monopsony will pay women lower wages if the female supply curve is less elastic than that for males. However, as Blau (1984) points out, "the persuasiveness of this explanation for aggregate pay differentials by sex is unclear, a priori. . . It seems likely that the monopsony explanation is more applicable to specific occupations. . ." (pp. 56–57).[6]

Goldberg (1982) also offers an explanation of how wage differentials may persist in the long run. Goldberg reformulates the discrimination model in terms of nepotism in favor of a particular group (i.e., whites) rather than a taste for discrimination against a particular group (i.e., blacks, or women). Within this framework, Goldberg explains that while discriminating firms go out of business in the long run, the nepotistic firm can "coexist along side [taste] neutral firms in the long run," (p. 318). Goldberg concludes that the nepotism model is consistent with wage differentials that persist in both the short run and long run.

Shulman (1984) suggests an additional explanation of how discrimination may not be eliminated in the long run.

> If there is an excess supply of labor, the costs of discrimination posited by the free-market model will be attenuated if not eliminated. The hiring of qualified workers need not be foregone, search time need not be appreciably expanded nor wages raised if the competition for jobs is severe enough. Given the high levels of unemployment which have existed for the past decade, the free-market model faces a problem in reconciling this reality with the hypothesis that discrimination increases costs. In effect such a hypothesis presumes full employment. Competition in

the product market may increase the costs of
discrimination, but competition in the labor market
does exactly the opposite (p. 116).

Joll et al. (1983) also discuss how discrimination may persist if
"conditions of less than full employment" exist for considerable periods
of time (p. 146). Markets may be operating below full employment such
that inadequate demand in the product market would be a deterrent for
potential nondiscriminating firms to enter. Also, insufficient demand
would deter firms from training or bidding up the wages of workers from
group B. "On the whole, therefore, one would anticipate that without the
assumption of full employment the discrimination predicted by tastes
models will not everywhere be a transitory phenomenon" (Joll et al.
1983, p. 147).

Thus, the notion has been raised in the recent literature of the
possible link between overall labor market conditions and the relative
economic status of "B" (minority) workers. We return to this possibility
in Chapter III.

HUMAN CAPITAL MODEL

Much of the research investigating the existence of wage
discrimination against women, blacks, and other groups relies on the basic
framework of the human capital paradigm (Blaug 1976). The general
model postulates that individuals make investments — e.g., education, on-
the-job training, health care, job search — that enhance their skill and
productivity and, therefore, their labor market potential. Human capital
theory may be summarized by the following: in a competitive labor
market individuals are paid according to their marginal productivity.
Human capital investments made by individuals increase their skill and
productivity, thus, wages are dependent upon the amount of investment
undertaken by the individual. Using this framework, variations in income
across individuals may be attributed to variations in worker productivity,
which is reflected by varying amounts of human capital investments.

This approach has been used by Mincer (1974), Chiswick
(1974), Mincer and Polachek (1974), and others to derive the now

familiar human capital earnings equation. The general form of the human capital earnings equation is:

(2-10) $\ln W = X\beta + \epsilon$

where W is earnings or wages and X is a set of explanatory variables that serve as proxies for human capital investments and ϵ is a stochastic error component. These variables include items such as years of formal schooling, years of potential labor market experience (often estimated as Age - Schooling - 5), experience squared, weeks worked, and other "ad hoc variables depending on the data used and specific purpose of the study" (Chiplin 1981, p. 988). Multivariate regression techniques are then used to estimate the parameters of this function over a sample of n observations.

Human capital analysis has been used to assess whether or not labor market discrimination exists against certain groups (e.g., women, blacks, the elderly, and various ethnic groups). In particular, human capital earnings functions (containing a vector of productivity related variables) are used to standardize for productivity differences between the two groups of workers in question. Using these estimated wage equations, researchers then measure the proportion of the wage differential that is accounted for by differences in productivity-related characteristics and attribute the residual to discrimination and other factors. (Criticisms of this approach are discussed in Chapter III.)

One method of empirically estimating the extent of wage discrimination is to examine the coefficient on a dummy variable used for sex, race, or ethnic differences. This method, however, is limited in that it assumes the explanatory variables have the same "impact" on wages for both groups (Blau, 1984, p. 62). A more common method (pioneered by Blinder 1973 and Oaxaca 1973) is to estimate the parameters of separate equations (like those in 2–10) for the groups in question. These equations may take the form:

(2–11) $\ln Y^A = X^A \beta'_A + \epsilon_A$ and
(2–12) $\ln Y^B = X_B \beta'_B + \epsilon_B,$

where A and B denote the two groups whose wages are to be examined. A basic property of multivariate regression analysis yields estimated equations of the form:

(2–13) $\overline{lnY^A} = \overline{X^A}\beta_A$ and

(2–14) $\overline{lnY^B} = \overline{X^B}\beta_B$

where $\overline{lnY^A}$ and $\overline{lnY^B}$ are the mean earnings of the two groups, B'$_A$ and B'$_B$ denote the estimated parameters for both groups, and $\overline{X^A}$ and $\overline{X^B}$ denote the mean values of the productivity-related explanatory variables for A and B workers, respectively. The assumption of a perfectly competitive labor market might imply identical coefficients across the two earnings equations, suggesting equal rewards for human capital investments made by workers in both groups (Filer, 1985). This implies that in the absence of discrimination, both A and B workers would be paid according to the same earnings structure (e.g., the A earnings function). Given their average characteristics, B workers are expected to have mean earnings equal to $\overline{lnY^{*B}} = \beta_A(\overline{X^B})$. Hence, the difference $\overline{lnY^A} - \overline{lnY^{*B}}$ is the difference in average earnings attributable to differences in mean values of personal characteristics. If, for example, this difference exceeds zero, the difference in characteristics favors A workers. The residual portion of the earnings difference is estimated by (that is, the difference in the constant terms plus the sum of the differences in regression coefficients, each weighted by the corresponding mean value for groups B). It is this unexplained residual portion of the wage gap that is often attributed to discrimination (Blinder 1973; Oaxaca 1973).

EMPIRICAL FINDINGS

A seminal work that utilized the residual approach to measuring wage discrimination was a study by Oaxaca (1973). Oaxaca used data from the 1967 Survey of Economic Opportunity and found a female/male earnings ratio of 54% for whites and 49% for blacks. He then estimated a human capital wage model for each of the four groups (black and white males, and black and white females). These estimated human capital wage models were then used in the wage decomposition method in such a way that the "effects of discrimination [were] approximated by the residual left after subtracting the effects of differences in individual characteristics from the overall wage differential" (Oaxaca 1973, p. 704). His calculations showed that for whites, discrimination accounts for 58.4

percent of the logarithmic male/female wage differential while for blacks 55.6 percent.

In a similar vein, Blinder (1973) independently employed the decomposition method in analyzing the white male/female and male black/white wage gap to data from the 1967 Michigan Survey Center's Panel Study of Income Dynamics. He estimated human capital wage models for each of the groups using the following variables: age, job tenure, education, health status, union membership, occupation, region (dummy variables accounting for the Northeast, North central, South, and West regions of the U.S.), local labor market conditions (dummy variables accounting for low unemployment, high unemployment, low wages, high wages) among other variables.

In explaining the 50.5 percent wage differential between white and black males, Blinder found that the major factors contributing to the wage advantage of white men over their black counterparts were higher levels of education by white males, and larger gains by whites from experience in the labor force (pp. 444–445). When decomposing this wage differential, Blinder found approximately 40 percent may be attributable to wage discrimination.[7]

In his study, Blinder also found a 45.6 percent "raw" wage differential for white males over white females. Factors favoring men included a more pronounced age-wage profile (i.e., the fact that men's wages rise more rapidly over the life-cycle), as well as education (men receive "much larger wage increments for advancing to higher education levels" (p. 448), and local labor market conditions (men's wages are less sensitive to conditions in the local labor market (p. 449)).[8] When applying the wage decomposition method, Blinder found approximately two thirds of the wage differential was attributable to wage discrimination in the labor market.

Gwartney and Long (1978) focused their study on the relative earnings of blacks and other minorities using data from the 1970 U.S. Census 1-in-100 Public Use Samples. They control for the variables education, age (as a proxy for experience), marital status, and location and residence (through the use of dummy variables). Gwartney and Long then estimate the portion of the minority/white wage difference that is not attributable to differences in personal characteristics. For black males, they estimate a 36 percent black/white male wage gap, of which 52.5 percent is estimated as being unexplained by differences in endowments of personal characteristics. For black females relative to white females, they conclude that 72.5 percent of the estimated 19 percent wage gap cannot be explained by productivity differences.

Carlson and Swartz (1988) extended Gwartney and Long's analysis using 1980 Census data from urban areas of twenty selected states. Since their study replicated that of Gwartney and Long, they followed the methodology of Gwartney and Long and did not correct for sample selection bias (see Chapter IV). Thus, they were able to compare their results with those of Gwartney and Long. As they note, "An important part of our research is a comparison of the relative earnings of women and members of ethnic minorities in 1979 with their relative earnings in 1959 and 1969" (Carlson and Swartz 1988, p. 531).

Carlson and Swartz found that during the 1970's the earnings of all minority men rose relative to those of white men. Upon examining the trend from 1959 to 1979, they noted that all the relative earnings of all minority males had risen and the unexplained residuals from the wage decomposition analysis had fallen. In comparing the relative earnings of minority women with those of white women, they found a narrowing of the earnings gap and a reduction in the unexplained portion of that gap. This led them to conclude that labor market experience for women of different races and ethnic backgrounds is becoming increasingly homogeneous (p. 544). When comparing the earnings of minority and white women with those of white men, however, Carlson and Swartz found different results. Their results suggest that all but two groups (white and Puerto Rican women) experienced gains in relative earnings between 1969 and 1979. Relative to white men, white women's earnings in 1979 remained at approximately the same level as in 1969. Carlson and Swartz postulate that the stagnation of white women's earnings may have been caused by the rapid increase in their labor force participation during the 1970's, although they concede that specific tests are needed for this hypothesis.

Another study illustrating the residual method of measuring discrimination was conducted by Corcoran and Duncan (1979). Corcoran and Duncan employed data from the 1976 Panel Study of Income Dynamics on 5212 household heads and spouses who were in the labor force in 1975 to investigate earnings differences between white men, black and white women, and black men. In comparing average wages, they found average wages for black men, white women and black women to be 77, 64, and 57 percent of those of white men. Among the independent variables included in their earnings equations are years of schooling, work experience, labor force attachment, and geographical residence. They found that, for black males, differences in productivity account for 53 percent of the wage gap. For white women, the explained portion of the male/female wage gap is 44 percent, while for black women they find only 32 percent of the wage gap explained by differences in productivity.

Reimers (1983) also employed the wage decomposition method to estimate the sources of the relative wage difference of Hispanic and black men. In estimating the wage structure of each group, Reimers included the explanatory variables; education (in the U.S. and abroad), potential work experience, nativity and date of immigration, U.S. military service, fluency in English, and health disability. In addition, Reimers also included the inverse of the Mills ratio to correct for sample selection bias. This last term (predicted from a sample-inclusion probit) "corrects for the expected error in the wage, given that the person worked, so that his wage is observed" (Reimers 1983, pp. 571–572).[9] Reimers used data from the 1976 Survey of Income and Education to regress the logarithm of real wages (equal to the nominal wage divided by a cost of living index for place of residence) on the set of explanatory variables. The results were then used to decompose the wage gap into the explained and residual portions. Of the 22 percent wage gap between non-Hispanic black and white men, Reimers found 58 percent to be unrelated to measured productivity differences. Similarly, of the 11 percent wage gap for Cuban males, 15.4 percent was found to be unexplained by productivity differences, while for Mexicans 15 percent of the 28 percent wage gap was unexplained.

O'Neill (1985) examined the recent trend in the male/female wage gap and investigated what factors may account for this trend. When tracing the "female-to-male" earnings ratio (from Census data) over time, O'Neill found that, in general, the ratio "follows a U-shaped path between 1955 and 1982" (p. S94). Upon closer examination (using both Current Population Reports from the Census Bureau and cohort information from National Longitudinal Survey data), O'Neill observed a fall in the level of education obtained by working women relative to the education level of men (p. S114). In addition, the rise in the labor force participation rate of women resulted in an increase in the number of new, older, less skilled entrants into the female labor force (as well as the baby boom cohort entrants) — an occurrence which would lead to a decline in the average level of work experience of employed women (p. S93, p. S114).[10] These two changes — the fall in the relative level of education and work experience of women — would lead to an increase in the pay gap between men and women. O'Neill notes, however, that "since these changes were sufficient to produce a larger widening in the pay gap than observed, labor market discrimination against women may, in fact, have declined" (p. S93).

A subsequent study by O'Neill and Polacheck (1993) examined the gender wage gap during the 1980's. Using data from the current Population Survey, Panel Study of Income Dynamics and the National Longitudinal Survey, they found an approximately 1% annual narrowing of the female/male wage gap since 1976. Contributing to this narrowing were factors such as an increase in women's work related characteristics (especially education and work experience), as well as higher returns to labor market experience. O'Neill and Polacheck point out that it is unclear whether the increase in human capital investments have occurred "because of women's own efforts, employer responses to women's increased work attachment, or a decline in discrimination," but note that these investments are long-term investments and, thus, should contribute to a continued narrowing of the gender wage gap (p. 225).

The 1980's, however, saw a widening of the black/white earnings differential (Saunders 1995, Darity and Myers 1993). Saunders found that the relative earnings of black men fell in each of the nine census regions during the 1980's. She found that black men experienced larger falls in relative incomes in regions where they were more concentrated (p. 71). For both white and black men, she found a decline in employment in higher earnings industries and in the lower paying industries, she found the earnings for white men rose relative to their black male counterparts (p. 71).

In many of the studies surveyed here (Oaxaca 1973, Blinder 1973, Corcoran and Duncan 1979, Gwartney and Long 1978, Reimers 1983) the emphasis was on the human capital approach to analyzing wage discrimination. This approach concentrates on differences in productivity-related characteristics among individuals and generally assumes that all workers participate in a common aggregate labor market (Hanushek 1981). An implication of competitive labor market theory is that within a common labor market, there will be a tendency "for labor of the same quality to obtain parity of net advantages" (Addison and Siebert 1979, p. 330). If there is free movement of factors of production, movement should take place so that equalization of relative factor payments across regions occurs. The culmination of this reasoning implies that the entire U.S. can be viewed as a single labor market.

Recent studies, however, provide empirical support for the proposition that there exist regional differences in wages which may, in fact, result from the existence of regional sub-labor markets such as states, counties, or cities (see Hanushek 1981, Hirsch 1978, Topel 1987). In typical discrimination studies, the approach used to account for the existence of regional variations in earnings is the inclusion of regional dummy variables (e.g., Census regions); as examples see Oaxaca 1973, Blinder 1973, Gwartney and Long 1978, and O'Neill 1985.[11] This empirical procedure, however, suffers from similar limitations as pointed out by Blau (1984) with respect to use of sex dummy variables. That is, in using these types of dummy variables, the influence that other explanatory variables have on wages is equated for the different groups (i.e., for males and females). In the case presented here, the use of dummy variables in accounting for regional variations implicitly equates the influence that other explanatory variables (e.g., education, experience, etc.) have on wages across the different regions.

In his 1978 study, Hirsch investigated whether or not returns to human capital variables differ across labor markets. Hirsch used 48 SMSA's to denote 48 different local labor markets, because the SMSA "most closely corresponds to the concept of a unified labor market on which the theory is based" (Hirsch 1978, p. 367). Utilizing a sample taken from the 1970 1-in-100 Census Public Use Sample, Hirsch estimates a simple version of the human capital earnings equation of the form:

$$(2-15) \quad \ln Y_i = r_o + rS_i + rt_i + rt_i^2 + \delta(\ln WW_i) + U_i$$

where Y_i is annual earnings of individual i. S_i is years of schooling completed by individual i, t_i is estimated labor market experience of individual i, WW_i is weeks worked by individual, and U_i is a stochastic error term. This equation is estimated using data on 62,411 white males residing in the 48 SMSA's. Separate earnings equations are then estimated for each of the 48 SMSA's. Hirsch used these regression results to calculate an F statistic for testing whether or not the sets of coefficients are homogeneous. He found the parameters of the simple human capital model to vary significantly across SMSA's and concluded that differences in average rates of return to schooling, earnings-experience profiles and the earnings-weeks worked relationship exist across U.S. labor markets. Moreover, in examining the ability of the human capital model (with its parameters fixed across labor markets) to explain earnings distributions within SMSA's, Hirsch found the human capital model to be "limited in its ability to predict distributions of earnings close to actual distributions" (p. 381). In comparing earnings distributions across SMSA's, Hirsch did not, however, take into account cost of living differences across those areas.

Hanushek's study (1981) concentrated on local labor market earnings determination for 341 distinct local markets (defined as SMSA's or County Groups if not an SMSA). He then estimated two separate earnings functions for each market using the data from the 1970 1-in-100 Public Use Sample for those white males with an education of high school or less (schooling $\leq$ 12 years) and for those white males with more than a high school education (schooling > 12 years). Aggregating these local markets by Census regions, Hanushek finds: (1) "substantial variation" in the schooling coefficients (p. 247); (2) mean earnings gains from additional schooling are higher for the more educated (schooling > 12 years) than for the less educated group (p. 247); and (3) "similar variations (not shown) for the experience parameters, although the variation appears quantitatively smaller. . . The important point is again that significant interactions between the shape of the earnings profile and local labor markets are observed" (p. 248). In conclusion Hanushek stated, "significant earnings differences — both in the level and shape of earnings profiles — exist across local labor markets. These findings cast considerable doubt on the assumption of homogeneous aggregate labor markets common to most past earnings analysis" (p. 249).

Local labor market differences in earnings and earnings profiles introduce questions about the interpretation of past earnings analysis. At any time, local labor markets exhibit sizable variations in structural aspects (e.g., in education and age distributions of the labor force, in the demand for labor, in unemployment rates, and in the occupational and industrial composition of employment (Hanushek 1981, Hyclack and Johnes 1987)), all of which may influence the structure of earnings across these labor markets.[12] Thus, wage discrimination studies assuming an aggregate labor market may be masking the effects of local labor markets on wages and, hence, on wage discrimination. If, as Hirsch and Hanushek suggest, a common U.S. labor market is inappropriate, then studies of local labor markets may be more appropriate. In particular, it is of interest to analyze what effects, if any, differences in local labor market conditions have on the estimates of labor market discrimination against women and blacks.

OCCUPATIONAL SEGREGATION

Another source of potential labor market discrimination against workers is occupational segregation (also known as occupational discrimination or labor market segmentation). The definition of occupational segregation used here is based on Becker's (1971) notion of segregation:

> . . .In general, if various members of different factors (such as laborers and foremen) are combined into one group by a criterion such as color or religion [or sex], one can say that market segregation of this group exists if its members are employed with each other to a significantly greater extent than would result from a random distribution of all members of each factor (pp. 56-57).

It is reasonable to anticipate that, in the absence of discrimination, the occupational distributions of workers are based on the productivity distributions of these groups. For example, if occupation k required a certain skill level (MP_k), rational employers would assign workers with requisite skills to this job. Discriminating employers, however, only hire B workers for jobs in the skill structure where the marginal product (MP_B) is more than the wage paid (w_B) by an amount no less than its discrimination coefficient d_B (Joll et al. 1983, p. 147). That is, workers from group B are assigned jobs such that:

(2–16) $w_B = w_k = Mp_k = MP_B - d_B.$

Thus, workers from group B will be employed some steps in the job structure below their potential, meaning that these workers may tend to be over represented in menial (presumably low pay) jobs (Bergmann 1971; Brown et al. 1980; Chiplin and Sloan 1976; Beller 1982).

This model is an extension of the employer taste for discrimination model for wage discrimination. Here, rather than employing B workers to their highest valued use (MP_B) and paying them a lower wage than corresponding A workers, it is assumed that A and B workers within the same occupation are paid the same wage, yet B workers are employed in jobs below their potential.

Much of the empirical work in assessing the extent of occupational segregation against minorities and women comes from a comparison of the percentage of male (white) workers and the percentage of female (minority) workers in various occupations.[13] Researchers such as Blau and Ferber (1992), Beller (1982; 1985) and England (1981) have noted that approximately two thirds of all women (or men, or some combination of the two) would have to change jobs for the occupational distributions of the two groups to be the same. On the other hand, estimates for minorities (for example blacks and Hispanics) suggest that 25 to 45 percent of the workers would have to change occupations to equalize the two distributions (see Blau and Ferber 1992; Westcott 1982; Llyson 1985; Gabriel , Williams, and Schmitz 1990 as examples).

In a recent study, Westcott (1982) found an improvement in the occupational distribution of blacks during the 1970's. Although proportionately more blacks moved into white collar occupations, she discovered that few had penetrated professional and managerial jobs. Westcott also noted that within blue-collar, service and farming jobs, blacks moved out of unskilled occupations into higher paying craft jobs. Expansion into higher paying jobs occurred predominately among black men residing in suburbs and nonmetropolitan areas. Among blacks living in the central city areas, the most progress was achieved by women.

In a similar vein, Beller (1985) examined changes in sex segregation that occurred during the 1970's. She found that occupational segregation against women declined more during the 1970's than during the 1960's. Using various data sources (1970 Census, Current Population Surveys (CPS), and Bureau of Labor Statistics) for different subperiods (1960–1970, 1971–1974, 1974–1977, and 1977–1981), Beller discovered that much of the decline came from women advancing into "nontraditional" white collar (especially managerial) occupations. On the other hand, she found predominantly male (blue-collar, craft) occupations and predominantly female (clerical) jobs remained highly segregated during the seventies. Similar conclusions have been reported by Blau and Ferber (1992) and Burris and Wharton (1982).

Albelda (1986) examined trends in occupational segregation by race and sex over the period 1958–1981. Using annual data from the Department of Labor for 29 occupations, she compares the occupational distributions for various gender-race subgroups. She finds that, holding race constant, the occupational distributions of all men and women have changed very little over the 24 year time span, while the greatest change has been in the distribution of nonwhite women relative to that of white women. In 1958, 50 percent of white or black women would have had to change jobs in order for the two distributions to be equal, compared to 17 percent in 1981. Occupational segregation between white and nonwhite men also declined during this time period. The occupational dissimilarity between white men and nonwhite women was the largest in all years, ahead of that between white men and women. Albelda concludes that changes in occupational segregation by gender have been small, whereas improvements by race have been substantial.

Albelda then used regression analysis to evaluate the relative importance of structural changes, education and the business cycle in determining changes in occupational distributions over the same time period. The two variables, time (a vector of 1 through 24) and its square (time-squared), are used to capture the effects of structural changes in the economy (e.g., affirmative action laws) on occupational segregation. Albelda speculates that with the advent of anti-discrimination legislation, occupational segregation should decline over time. Therefore, she hypothesizes the sign on the time coefficient to be negative. The variable time squared tests for nonlinearity in job distribution trends. Albelda argues that a positive (negative) sign on this coefficient would indicate that the occupational distributions of the groups converged (diverged) more rapidly during the earlier portion of the 24 year period. The general unemployment rate is used as a proxy for measuring cyclical variations over the time span. Albelda hypothesizes that during periods of low unemployment, women and nonwhites may gain access into occupations from which they have previously been excluded. This suggests that the hypothesized sign on the unemployment coefficient is negative.

The results of the model for various race and gender subgroups suggest that, holding education and the business cycle constant, the dissimilarity between the male and female occupational distributions is positively correlated with time while the opposite is true for occupational comparisons by race (p. 4120). This leads Albelda to conclude that structural changes may have "impeded" occupational convergence by gender (p. 410). With respect to education, Albelda finds that holding gender constant, educational attainment helped nonwhites gain access to traditionally white jobs. She also found that fluctuations in unemployment affect the relative occupational distributions of women and nonwhites since the sign on the unemployment variable had the predicted sign in all equations.

King (1992) expanded upon Albelda's work by focusing on a longer time period, 1940–88, and using more detailed occupational breakdowns. Her results of gender segregation are comparable to other authors but indicate greater segregation than Albelda's results (pp. 33–34). The results for occupational segregation by race show that the index of dissimilarity fell over the 48 year period with the most significant changes occurring during the 1960's and 1970's (p. 33). For women, the largest decline occurred during the 1970's.

If factors such as education and unemployment influence the relative occupational distributions of minority groups, then it is of interest to examine the influence such variables have within the context of a local labor market.

SUMMARY

Numerous studies analyzing the existence and extent of occupational segregation and wage discrimination against women and minorities aggregate workers into a national data set. This implicitly assumes all workers are participating in an aggregate labor market. The empirical analyses of Hirsch, Hanushek, Topel and others cast doubt on the assumption of homogeneous aggregate labor markets. Hence, past studies may have omitted an important consideration: the relationship between local labor market heterogeneity and the economic status of minorities and women.

This study expands previous empirical works in the area of labor market discrimination by: (1) incorporating different wage and occupational structures across local labor markets; and (2) assessing the effect that local labor market conditions have on conventional estimates of wage and occupational discrimination against women and blacks. The next chapter provides an operational definition of a local labor market and explains how the relative economic status of women and blacks might be influenced by local market conditions such as unemployment. Finally, a general model is developed from which certain hypotheses are to be formulated and tested.

III

Local Labor Markets and Discrimination

INTRODUCTION

The primary focus of this study is to analyze the possible impact that differences in local labor market conditions have on estimates of labor market discrimination against women and black males. Chapter II showed how the competitive wage model could be extended to analyze labor market discrimination and presented an overview of some of the more important works in the area of labor market discrimination. This chapter explains how the relative economic status of women and blacks may be influenced by local market conditions.

APPROPRIATE DEFINITION OF A LABOR MARKET

The concept of a competitive labor market is an integral part of the basic neoclassical wage determination model. The definition of a competitive labor market can be found in most labor economics texts. For example, McConnell and Brue (1995) list the following salient features of a competitive market for labor services: (1) a large number of firms competing with one another to hire a specific type of labor to fill identical jobs; (2) numerous qualified people who have identical skills and who independently supply their labor services; (3) wage-taking behavior by firms and workers; and (4) costless information and labor mobility (p. 155).

Wage studies that use national samples implicitly assume that the aggregate U.S. labor market approximates the competitive ideal. As Hirsch (1978) and Hanushek (1981) have pointed out, however, significant differences exist across local labor markets, thus warranting additional inquiry into wage disparities across local markets. This issue is particularly relevant in studying the economic status of minorities. Fujii and Mak (1983) address this when examining the economic status of ethnic minorities in Hawaii. They find that their estimates of the earnings structures of certain ethnic groups in Hawaii (e.g., Japanese, Chinese, and Filipino) differ from Chiswick's (1983) estimates for the U.S. as a whole

(p. 775). Fujii and Mak argue that minorities may face different earnings and occupational opportunities, as well as varying degrees of discrimination in different labor markets. Their results suggest that empirical analyses conducted within the context of a local labor market may be better suited to examining relative wage and occupational differentials between groups of workers.

An examination of the relative economic status of minorities across local labor markets is contingent upon defining what is meant by a local labor market. From an employer's point of view, Derek Robinson [as quoted by Goodman (1970)] defines a local labor market to be a "geographical area containing those members of the labor force, or potential members of the labor force that a firm can induce to enter its employ under certain conditions," and containing "those employees with whom the firm is in competition for labor" (Goodman 1970, p. 83). From the worker's point of view, it "may consist only of those jobs (within or outside the present firm) about which he hears, which meet his preconceptions of his ability to obtain and retain them" (Goodman 1970, p. 183). Also involved in determining the worker's view of a local market are the worker's locational preferences which include the "places at which the worker is willing to work, how he gets there from his residence and also the time spent in the journey to work" (Goldner 1955, p. 114). Thus, within a local labor market, the spatial distribution of the demand for labor is expressed by the location of the workplaces, and the supply of labor by the location of residences as determined by the worker's preferences with respect to work, commuting time and leisure time (Goodman 1970, Goldner 1955).

Goodman (1970) uses the above general criteria in an attempt to establish a specific operational definition of a local labor market. His definition concentrates on an area in which a number of employers and employees have in common. Such an area must also meet two requirements: (1) it must be a spatially defined area, the boundary of which is rarely crossed in daily journeys to work; and (2) it should possess a high degree of intra-market movement (p. 184). This latter criteria implies that workers primarily search for jobs in that area, and employers primarily search for employees from within that area. In a similar vein, Hyclak and Johnes (1987) adopted the concept of a local labor market as outlined by the Pennsylvania Department of Labor. This says that a local labor market is "an economically integrated geographic unit within which workers may readily change jobs without changing their place of residence" (p. 193).

The notion of a local labor market presented by these analysts seems to closely adhere to the concept of a competitive market. If an area is to approximate a competitive market model, it must be largely self-sufficient in both labor supply and employment, and display a high volume of labor mobility within its boundaries (Goodman 1970, p. 184). Neoclassical economic theory predicts that, for a given labor market, a market wage will emerge, via the classical competitive process, for a given form of labor service at full employment.

Although conceptually difficult to illustrate, it may be possible to determine an empirically operational form of the local labor market definition outlined above. Perhaps most closely resembling the local labor market definition is the Standard Metropolitan Statistical Area, (SMSA), because the SMSA contains "both the supply and demand components that determine factor incomes, and it possesses a high degree of labor mobility within its boundaries" (Hirsch 1978, p. 367).

The concept of an SMSA encompasses a metropolitan area with "a large population nucleus, together with adjacent communities, which have a high degree of economic and social integration with that nucleus" (Census 1984, p. A1). The criteria for an SMSA (as developed by the interagency Federal Committee on Standard Metropolitan Statistical Areas) includes: one or more central counties containing the area's main population concentration; an urbanized area with a minimum of 50,000 inhabitants; and a total SMSA population of at least 100,000 (or in New England 75,000). An SMSA may also include outlying counties which have close social and economic ties with the central counties (Census 1984, p. A1). To be included, the outlying counties must have a specified level of commuting to the central county and must meet certain requirements with respect to "metropolitan character" such as population density, metropolitan population, and population growth (Census 1984, p. A2). In New England, SMSA's are composed of cities and towns rather than whole counties.

From the above definition of an SMSA, we choose to assume that within a given SMSA large and small firms compete for a specific labor service from a local labor pool and that labor is mobile within the SMSA. The SMSA is preferred to other representations of a local labor market, such as a county, since workers often cross county lines in their journey to work. The SMSA also provides a working definition of the local labor market that is easily implemented in empirical research (especially on a national level). Using the SMSA, it is possible to examine the effects that local labor market conditions have on relative wages and occupational structures of groups such as blacks and women.

At any given time, geographically dispersed labor markets vary in characteristics such as unemployment rates. Causes of these regional disparities have often been attributed to specific industry characteristics (caused by changing product markets or technology), uneven effects of national cyclical forces across regions, changes in local demand for labor, or differences in frictional unemployment due to the geographic immobility of labor (for a discussion see Topel 1987, 1984; Hyclak and Johnes 1987; Iden 1967; Murphy 1985; Murphy and Hofler 1984; Behaman 1978 as examples). Table 3.1 illustrates some specific factors cited in the literature that affect local disparities in unemployment rates.

Table 3.1
Some Factors Affecting Unemployment Rate Disparities
(Direction of the Effect)

Factor	Author
weak employment growth (+)	Topel (87)
accelerating out-migration of young, more educated workers (+)	Topel (87)
rapid increase in labor force participation rates of women and blacks (+)	Beham (78) Iden (67)
proportion of employment in manufacturing (+)	Iden (67) Beham (78)
Proportion of labor force in white collar occupations (-)	Iden (67)
% unionized within labor market (p. 119) (+)	Hirsch and Addison (86)
% of working age population that is non-white (+)	Murphy (85) Murphy and Hofler (84)
proportion of working age population possessing at least a high school degree (may be + or -)	Murphy (85) Beham (78)

POSSIBLE LINK BETWEEN DISCRIMINATION AND LABOR MARKET CONDITIONS

As discussed in the previous section, local labor markets display such diversity in terms of economic conditions that many researchers have adopted the practice of categorizing labor markets as being "tight" or "loose." Although these classifications are frequently used in the literature, there seems to be no specific definition as to what classifies a labor market as being tight or loose. Ehrenberg and Smith (1994) provide the following basic criteria: A tight labor market "indicates that jobs in general are plentiful and hard for employers to fill and that most of those who are unemployed will find other work quickly" (p. 29). On the other hand, a loose (or slack) labor market is one in which, "workers are abundant and jobs are relatively easy for employers to fill" (p. 29). This general definition has appeared elsewhere in the literature (see Tobin 1965, p. 880 as an example).

To illustrate how discrimination may persist as labor market conditions deteriorate, the following explanation is offered. Assume a labor market is characterized as being loose and thus providing low employment opportunities. There are two groups of workers, A and B, who are equally productive. B workers, however, receive unequal treatment in the labor market because firms operate with a taste for discrimination against them. Given the slack market, discriminating firms who are engaged in layoffs may give preference to those workers from group A in the layoff decision. The growing firm, looking to hire workers, can now "pick and choose, both in recruiting and promoting" (Tobin 1965, p. 883). Firms that are now hiring or promoting workers for a given occupation find that the applicant pool is being saturated with workers from group A (given the abundant supply of workers in the market). Qualified workers from group B who have moved up the hiring and promotion queue are "bumped" back as firms give preference to those workers from group A (Shulman 1987, p. 365). Discriminating firms would no longer have to hire less productive individuals from group A nor offer as large wage premiums to attract those A workers who are qualified. Equally qualified workers from group B who have been "bumped" in the queue would now face higher unemployment rates and tend to be found in lower paying occupations (Tobin 1965). Without access to the same opportunities the relative wage and occupational differential between the two groups would worsen. The discriminating firm operating in this type of labor market finds that "increased unemployment will reduce the costs of discrimination" (Shulman 1987, p. 365).

In terms of worker (employee) discrimination, loose labor market conditions may also increase the propensity to discriminate. In labor markets characterized by conditions such as high unemployment rates, workers place a premium on job security. Workers from group A realize the significance of informal job distribution channels (i.e., inside information) as the availability of jobs declines. With a taste for discrimination existing against workers from group B, A workers may refuse to share job information with workers from group B. Thus, workers from group A have better access to such job information. Workers from group A would benefit from solidarity as they pressure the firm to discriminate against B workers in personnel decisions (such as hiring, training, promotion, and layoff). In such a situation the discriminating firm might experience reduced unit labor costs by lowering wages of all workers and raising productivity through establishing a cooperative relationship with its group A workforce. As unemployment worsens, firms will be less likely to increase group B hires and promotions and more willing to reserve occupational opportunities for A workers (Shulman 1987, p. 365).

A more radical view of how discrimination may worsen in a loose labor market is offered by Reich (1981) and Shulman (1987). This view contends that the firm itself may instigate increased discrimination to reduce the bargaining power of workers from group A. This may be achieved by the firm threatening to replace the A workers with those from group B, given the plentiful supply of available workers. The firm may take this approach since increased unemployment reduces the costs of discrimination. In this case, unemployment again acts to deteriorate the relative economic position of workers from group B.

A slack labor market may also contribute to a decline in the economic status of blacks and women relative to white men, since institutional factors (such as seniority provisions) may affect the groups differently. During periods of high unemployment, women and blacks may be fired or not hired for certain occupations since they have less seniority or less experience than their white male counterparts.

Turning to the case of a tight labor market, if the firm finds itself in a position to hire or promote workers for a certain occupation, it would first attempt to recruit workers from group A. However, because of the restricted supply of these workers, the firm finds it more difficult to recruit A workers at the prevailing wage. As the discriminating firm continues its search for A workers, it will find itself operating with a less productive workforce (in bypassing qualified workers from group B) or with higher labor costs. Given the increased search time and delay required in hiring workers from group A, the firm may eventually lean towards hiring workers from group B. With the tight labor market firms would compete for qualified B workers, thereby raising the wage rate of workers in group B.[1] As the wage rate of B workers increases it may start to approach that of workers in group A, leading to a possible narrowing of the wage differential between the two groups and a possible decline in wage discrimination against workers in group B. In a labor market characterized by tight economic conditions, the costs of discrimination have increased such that only nondiscriminating firms should survive in the long run -- a conclusion predicted by the models of Becker (1971) and Arrow (1972, 1973). The role of tight labor markets in increasing the costs of discrimination has also been noted by other economists (see Heckman and Payner 1989; Reder 1973; McCall 1972; Tobin 1965; Friedman 1962 as a few examples).

Under tight labor market conditions, workers from group B are more likely to move into higher paying occupations and receive increasing wages (Tobin 1965, p. 884). This point is emphasized by Shulman (1987) with respect to blacks,

> . . . Improvements in relative black education will therefore only pay off in improvements in employment and on-the-job training if the labor market is tight enough to allow blacks to move up the hiring queue and to penalize discriminators. The link between education, employment, and training is thus mediated by the overall rate of unemployment (p. 365).

Shulman's contention that the costs of discrimination are inversely related to the degree of tightness of the labor market is not meant to displace neoclassical wage theory or human capital analysis. Rather, he suggests that the logic and conclusions of the theory depend upon the labor market context. Relative black earnings can increase with human capital acquisition, but the relative probability of employment and types of jobs acquired can at the same time deteriorate with increasing white unemployment. Increasing white unemployment in a slack labor market increases the competition for jobs and at the same time may increase the effects of discrimination against blacks (p. 365).

Shulman's argument concerning black/white differentials is echoed in a similar, although simplified, context by Reder (1973). Reder contends that in periods of economic growth, low white unemployment will increase the delay required to hire an additional white worker. Therefore, some firms resort to hiring blacks to avoid excessive delays in filling position. On the other hand, during recessionary periods, these employers might hire whites exclusively. Reder concludes that, "the relative labor market position of blacks and other victims of labor market discrimination varies in the same direction as the level of business activity" (1973, pp. 38–39).

Turning to the male/female wage gap, O'Neill (1985) offers an explanation of how cyclical fluctuations in unemployment may affect earnings differentials by sex. She notes that women are less likely than men to be covered by collective bargaining agreements, so that women's wages are likely to be more flexible relative to men's. This implies greater employment stability for women during a recession but also implies a possible widening of the male/female wage gap during such a recession (and vice-versa during an economic expansion). She claims another possibility is that within a given industry or occupation, women are likely to possess less "specific training" (i.e., training which increases the worker's productivity only in the firm providing that training) than men. This may result in their being more vulnerable to layoffs during recessions, implying a generally weaker labor market for women during economic slowdowns. "Both of these factors (less union coverage and less specific training) suggest a positive relation between unemployment and the pay gap, [while] working in the opposite direction, is women's concentration in occupations and industries with stable demand" (O'Neill 1985, p. S111).

O'Neill (1985) then examined what effect changes in unemployment may have on the male/female pay gap through the use of time series regressions over the period 1955–1982. To measure unemployment O'Neill chose to use the unemployment rate for married men, since the unemployment rate for married men is expected to be influenced less by the change in women's labor force entry than the overall unemployment rate (p. S112). Using the female-to-male earnings ratio as the dependent variable and the unemployment rate of married men, the male-female schooling differential and the percentage of female workers who are married as explanatory variables, O'Neill found that an increase in unemployment increases the wage gap (p. S112). However, her study makes use of a national data sample, thereby omitting the possible differences in wage structures that exist across local labor markets.

McCall (1972) echoes the notion that minorities tend to fare better as the labor market tightens. He notes that in a tight labor market, employers may be induced to engage in such "experiments" as hiring or promoting minorities as the number of qualified preferred workers searching for employment diminishes (p. 206). McCall offers that the outcomes of these "experiments" would alter any incorrect perceptions employers and employees may have toward minorities so that eventually in tight labor markets discrimination would decline in a "very natural way" (p. 206).

As the previous discussion indicates, many researchers tacitly support the proposition that the relative economic position of minority groups improves during economic upswings. Few, if any, have attempted to empirically assess whether changes in estimates of labor market discrimination are associated with changes in labor market conditions while accounting for different wage and occupational structures across local labor markets.

Our discussion suggests that differential treatment of minorities (e.g., discrimination) in the labor market might be accentuated by differing labor market conditions. In general, it is possible that minorities benefit from improving labor market conditions; and suffer when conditions deteriorate. If the U.S. is composed of many distinct local labor markets, then it is reasonable to assume that economic characteristics might vary across these local markets such that minorities fare better in those markets experiencing improving conditions. On the other hand, changes in local labor market conditions may affect all workers in the same way. If wage and occupational structures of minorities are affected in the same way as white males, we may find no systematic relationship between changes in our estimates of discrimination and changes in labor market conditions.

In the next section, a general model is developed that investigates the existence of labor market discrimination against women and blacks and how local labor market conditions may affect these estimates.

MODEL FORMULATION

This section's objective is twofold: (1) to outline general empirical methods of assessing the existence (and extent) of wage and occupational discrimination against women and blacks; and (2) to design a test capable of determining the effects that local labor market differences have on the estimates of discrimination. In general, this test should incorporate such local market characteristics as unemployment rates, local labor demand, local relative supply of minority workers (to name a few) and allow the analyst to assess the effect that each of the specified characteristics has on the estimates of discrimination.

Wage Discrimination. Becker's seminal work (1971) in the area of labor market discrimination stands as a springboard for empirical research in this area. Beginning with the assumption that there is a distribution of "tastes" for discrimination among employers in a particular labor market, Becker derives the market wage discrimination coefficient. The discrimination coefficient (D) is the difference between an individual's marginal contribution to output and their wage. In the presence of discrimination, the coefficient D can be defined in terms of the first order maximizing conditions for inputs (Butler 1982):

$$(3\text{–}1) \qquad \frac{MP_B}{MP_A} = D \, \frac{w_B}{w_A} \, .$$

where subscript A denotes the preferred worker, B the minority worker, MP_A and MP_B their marginal products respectively, w_A and w_B their wages, and D the market discrimination factor. In logarithmic form expression (3–1) becomes:

$$(3\text{–}2) \qquad \ln w_A - \ln w_B = \ln MP_A - \ln MP_B + \ln D.$$

Given the specification of the discrimination coefficient in equations (3-1) and (3–2), the next step undertaken by researchers was to estimate D from labor market data. This proved problematic empirically because factors such as the market wage and workers' marginal productivities are not directly observable.

As noted in the previous chapter, subsequent research by Oaxaca (1973) and Blinder (1973) attempted to empirically estimate the magnitude of the discrimination coefficient against various groups.

Oaxaca and Blinder suggested a technique that decomposes the observed wage differentials between groups of workers into two components: one based on intergroup productivity differentials (the so-called endowment effect) and a second that represents the residual component, what analysts frequently attribute as an upper bound estimate to the extent of wage discrimination (Chiplin 1973; Chiplin and Sloane 1976).

The Blinder/Oaxaca methodology may be adapted to ascertain the influence that local labor market conditions have on wage discrimination. For the general specification of the wage model for A and B workers it is assumed that the human capital earnings function is of the following form:

$$(3\text{-}3) \quad \ln w_A = X_a\beta_A + \epsilon_A \text{ and}$$
$$\ln w_B = X_b\beta_B + \epsilon_B$$

where w is earnings, X is a vector of characteristics that serve as proxies for productivity enhancing characteristics, β a vector of coefficients to be estimated, and ϵ_A and ϵ_B are stochastic error terms with mean zero and variance σ^2. It is assumed that in the absence of discrimination, B workers would be offered the same wages as A for equal characteristics. Substituting (3–3) into (3–1) results in the following expression:

$$(3\text{-}4) \quad \overline{\ln w_A} - \overline{\ln w_B} = \overline{X}_A\beta_A - \overline{X}_B\beta_B$$

where the denotes average log wage for the two groups, and $\overline{X}$ denotes personal characteristics evaluated at their mean values. If it is assumed that B workers are paid according to the A earnings structure, the wage differential can be modified into the form:[2]

$$(3\text{-}5) \quad \overline{\ln w_A} - \overline{\ln w_B} = (\overline{X}_A - \overline{X}_B)\beta_A + (\beta_A - \beta_B)\overline{X}_B.$$

The first term on the right-hand side of equation (3-5) corresponds to ln MP_A - ln MP_B — the portion of the wage differential attributable to differences in average productivity, while the second term corresponds to ln D — the unexplained portion of the wage differential that is frequently attributed to discrimination.

The general formulations given in expressions (3–3) through (3–5) should be interpreted as approximation techniques, rather than exact specifications for the underlying earnings structures of workers and estimates of discrimination. Recent research has enumerated several difficulties with earnings models such as (3–3). One problem with these formulations is that expression (3–3) is a reduced-form expression, incorporating both supply and demand forces (see Blaug 1976, 1980; McCrakin 1984; Butler 1982, 1983; Blau 1984). A second difficulty is that the X vector contains proxies for productivity rather than precise skill measures (Blaug 1976, 1980; Butler 1982; Blau 1984). Another criticism of this type of model lies with the interpretation of the residual component of the wage differential. This component may represent, in part, differences in the quality of the attributes (e.g., schooling) possessed by workers. These problems may bias the estimates produced by the Blinder/Oaxaca earnings decomposition method (Butler 1982, pp. 607–608). There is currently no proffered empirical specification, however, that overcomes these difficulties to such an extent that the human capital and decomposition approach to analyzing earnings differences among workers is rejected (Marshall 1974; Blaug 1980; Neumark 1988).[3]

The earnings model presented in expressions (3–3) through (3–5) may be adapted to discern the influence that local labor market conditions have on estimates of wage discrimination. Using the SMSA as the local labor market, an estimate for D may be calculated for each of the SMSA's included in the study. For convenience, we use an index, J, to represent the total number of SMSA's employed in this analysis.

A primary hypothesis investigated in this study is whether estimates of wage discrimination are influenced by local labor market conditions such as unemployment rates, relative supply of minorities, local labor demand, and other factors. Thus, conditions in each of the J SMSA's are examined for the period corresponding to the calculation of D. Given the observed characteristics of a particular labor market at a given point in time, one cannot immediately infer the state of the market. For example, an unemployment rate of 10 percent may be taken by some analysts to signal a slack labor market. If, however, that particular market has historically experienced unemployment rates in excess of 10 percent, then it may have instead been experiencing a labor market tightening. To circumvent this problem, we examine the change in each local labor market variable over a specified period of time. In the example, a decline in the unemployment rate would be taken as a signal that the labor market had tightened since the previous time period.

This procedure is, however, not without its limitations. In the absence of an absolute measure indicating whether a labor market is tight or loose, we rely on the direction of the change in economic variables.

This implies that labor markets experiencing, for example, extremely low or high values of variables such as unemployment rates, may undergo changes which are interpreted as a tightening or loosening of that particular labor market when, in fact, the market has not really tightened or loosened. For example, an increase in the unemployment rate from 3 to 4 percent in a labor market would be interpreted as though that particular labor market had loosened, yet many economists would still consider an unemployment rate of 4 percent as signaling a tight labor market.

In addition to observable economic heterogeneity, labor markets also feature unobservable heterogeneities which influence earnings or occupations. Possible examples of these types of unobserved factors include (but are not limited to) tastes with respect to labor force attachment or occupations, or nonpecuniary aspects of the local labor market (e.g., culture). Such factors are assumed to be constant for a given cross-sectional unit over time but may vary across cross-sectional units — where the J SMSA's represent the J cross-sectional units. A model that attempts to determine the effects of local labor market conditions on estimates of discrimination may thus suffer from biases resulting from omission of the unobservable variables. Since these factors are assumed invariant over time, the omitted variable bias may be minimized by employing a type of fixed effect model (Hsaio 1986, Chapters 3 and 7). Hsaio suggests a strategy whereby a differencing of the sample observations eliminates the individual (i.e., SMSA) specific but time-invariant effects (p. 214). Adopting this type of strategy to the problem at hand involves: (1) estimating the discrimination coefficient for all SMSA's for each specified time period; (2) determining the change in the estimated discrimination coefficient (D_j) that has taken place over the stipulated period of time; (3) determining changes in labor market conditions that may have occurred during that stipulated time; and (4) evaluating the relationship between (2) and (3).

In determining the change in D_j, a discrimination coefficient is calculated for each of the J SMSA's at time t (i.e., D_{jt}) and again for time t+n (i.e., $D_{j,\,t+n}$). The subsequent change between the two may be expressed as:

$$(3\text{–}6) \quad \Delta D_j = D_{j,\,t+n} - D_{jt}.$$

If ΔD_j is negative, this will be taken as an indication that the estimated level of wage discrimination has fallen in the jth SMSA over the specified time interval, n. Conversely, if ΔD_j is positive, this would imply that wage discrimination had worsened (increased) during that same time span.

Determining the change in local labor market conditions becomes more problematic. Unfortunately, there is no single measure that accurately portrays conditions prevailing in a labor market. Existing labor market conditions in time t may thus be expressed as Θ_{jt} — a vector of variables that are related to local labor market conditions in the jth SMSA.[4] Θ_{jt} can be stated as:

$$(3\text{--}7) \quad \Theta_{jt} = (\alpha_{1jt}, \alpha_{2jt}, \ldots, \alpha_{kjt}, \alpha_{k+1,j,t})$$

where $\alpha_{1jt}, \alpha_{2jt}, \ldots, \alpha_{kjt}$ represent the K factors reflecting labor market conditions in the jth SMSA in time t. The variable $\alpha_{k+1,j,t}$ represents an unobservable factor (unique to the jth (SMSA) that influences wages. For time period t+n, prevailing labor market conditions for the jth SMSA are expressed as $\Theta_{j,t+n}$ — a vector of the same variables as in (3–7) in time t+n.

For each of the J SMSA's, changes in local labor market conditions that have occurred during the n time periods may be expressed as:

$$(3\text{--}8) \quad \Delta\theta_j = \Theta_{j,.t+n} - \Theta_{jt}$$
$$= (\alpha_{1j,\,t+n} - \alpha_{1jt}, \alpha_{2j,t+n} - \alpha_{2jt}, \ldots,$$
$$\alpha_{kj,t+n} - \alpha_{kjt}, \alpha_{k+1,j,t+n} - \alpha_{k+1,j,t})$$
$$= (\Delta\alpha_{1j}, \Delta\alpha_{2j}, \ldots, \Delta\alpha_{kj,} \Delta\alpha_{k+1,j})$$

where $\Delta\alpha_{kj}$ represents changes in the K labor market variables that have occurred during the specific time and $\Delta\alpha_{k+1,j}$ equals zero.

Multiple regression analysis can then be used to assess the net effects of changes in the K labor market variables on the change in the wage discrimination coefficient. Equation (3–9) gives the general form of the model:

$$(3\text{--}9) \quad \Delta D_j = \pi_o + \pi_1\Delta\alpha_{ij} + \pi_2\Delta\alpha_{2j} + \ldots$$
$$+ \pi_k\Delta\alpha_{kj} + \pi_{k+1}\Delta\alpha_{k+1,j} + \epsilon,$$

which can be rewritten as:

$$= \pi_o + \pi_1\Delta\alpha_{1j} + \pi_2\Delta\alpha_{2j} + \ldots + \pi_k\Delta\alpha_{kj} + \epsilon$$

since $\Delta\alpha_{k+1,k}$ equals zero. The subscript j represents the observation unit (i.e., the SMSA). The total number of observations equals the total number of SMSA's. The resulting test hypotheses become

$$(3\text{-}10) \quad H_o = \frac{\delta\Delta D}{\delta\Delta\alpha_k} = \pi_k \underset{>}{\overset{<}{=}} 0.$$

Exact hypotheses are detailed in Chapters IV and V.

Ordinary least square estimation of the coefficients in equation (3–9) provide estimates of the direction of the relationship between the change in the local labor market variable ($\Delta\alpha_k$) and the change in wage discrimination against the minority group. As an example, suppose that α_1 is expressed as the unemployment rate for the preferred workers. If this unemployment rate rose during the specified time, we would expect competition for jobs to intensify so that employers may be able to fill their vacancies with the preferred workers (given the abundant supply of these workers). Employers would be less willing to employ or promote minority workers in this case. We would hypothesize that an increase in the unemployment rate for the preferred workers would thus be expected to increase our estimates of wage discrimination in the labor market (i.e, $\pi_1 > 0$).

Occupational Segregation. Attempts to understand the economic status of minority groups have often focused on the occupational structure of these groups. Occupational segregation refers to a situation where two groups of workers tend to work in a different set of occupations on the basis of nonproductivity factors (such as race or sex). One measure of occupational segregation that is frequently used in the literature is the index of dissimilarity (also known as the segregation index) (see, for example, Duncan and Duncan 1955; Miller and Volker 1985; Blau and Ferber 1992; King 1992). The index is based on the absolute differences between the proportion of workers from the preferred group (i.e., group A) in a particular occupational category and the proportion of minority workers (i.e., group B) holding jobs in the same category. The index of dissimilarity is defined as:

$$(3\text{-}11) \quad S = \frac{1}{2} \sum_{m=1}^{M} |P_{Am} - P_{Bm}|$$

where P_{AM} is the percentage of A workforce in occupation m, and P_{BM} is the percentage of B workforce in the same occupation m. Expression (3–11) is used to provide an objective measure of occupational segregation. The index (S) gives the percentage of A (or B) workers who would have to shift between jobs to equalize occupational distributions between the two groups. S can range from zero to one; a value of zero indicates that the distribution of the two groups of workers across occupational categories is identical, while a value of one indicates total segregation.

The index of dissimilarity, while representing a means of assessing occupational segregation, does suffer from certain limitations (for additional discussions of methodological issues surrounding the dissimilarity index see King 1992; Watts 1992, 1995). First, minorities may choose to be in a narrow range if occupations based on non-monetary considerations (e.g., taste). What may then appear as occupational segregation is instead reflecting rational job choice on the part of minorities. Second, if one SMSA has an index of dissimilarity that is twice the size of another, one might ask the question: Is the first SMSA twice as segregated as the second? This is a problem common to index numbers in general. A third problem with this approach to occupational segregation is one of data availability. Optimally, a measure of segregation would compare actual job applicants to a firm with those individuals the firm actually hires or promotes. However, such data of the magnitude required in this analysis are currently unavailable. Given available data, the index of dissimilarity does provide a measure, albeit imperfect, with which existing occupational distributions may be compared and corresponding inferences made.

To assess how the occupational structure of minorities changes with concurrent changes in local labor market conditions the following strategy is employed. First, the index of dissimilarity is calculated for each of the J SMSA's in time t (i.e., S_{jt}) and again for time t+n (i.e., $S_{j,t+n}$). The change between the two yields:

(3–12) $\Delta S_j = S_{j,t+n} - S_{jt}$.

If the change in the index is negative, this implies that the occupational distributions of the two groups have become more similar (a reduction in occupational segregation). An increase in the index implies that the two occupational distributions have become more dissimilar (an increase in occupational segregation) (Blau and Ferber 1986; Miller and Volker 1985). This procedure reduces the magnitude of the index number problem since the direction of the change in S is of relatively more importance than the actual numerical value itself.

Second, changes in local labor market conditions that have occurred during the specified time span (i.e., $\Delta\theta_j$) are determined for each SMSA following the same strategy as in the wage discrimination model. From expression (3–8) changes in local labor market conditions for the jth SMSA are expressed as:

$$\Delta\Theta_j = \theta_{j,t+n} - \theta_{jt}$$
$$= (\Delta\alpha_{1j}, \Delta\alpha_{2j}, \ldots, \Delta\alpha_{kj}, 0)$$

where $\Delta\alpha_{kj}$ represents changes in each of the K labor market variables that have occurred during the specific time span and zero, again, is the change in the unobserved factor.

To assess the direction of the relationship between changes in the K labor market variables and changes in the index of dissimilarity, multiple regression analysis may again be used. In this case, the change in the index of dissimilarity is the dependent variable while changes in the K labor market variables are the independent variables (an observation corresponds to an individual SMSA). The resulting model can be expressed as:

$$(3\text{–}14) \quad \Delta S_j = \tau_o + \tau_1\Delta\alpha_{1j} + \tau_2\Delta\alpha_{2j} + \ldots$$
$$+ \tau_k\Delta\alpha_{kj} + \epsilon.$$

The testable hypotheses thus become:

$$(3\text{–}15) \quad H_o = \frac{\delta\Delta S}{\delta\Delta\alpha_k} = \tau_k \overset{<}{\underset{>}{=}} 0.$$

Ordinary least square estimation of the coefficients in equation (3–14) provide estimates of the direction of the relationship between the change in the local labor market variable ($\Delta\alpha_k$) and the change in occupational segregation against the minority group. Referring back to the previous example, suppose that a_1 is the unemployment rate for the preferred workers. If this unemployment rate rose during the specified time, competition for jobs is expected to intensify so that employers may be able to fill their vacancies with workers from the preferred group (given the abundant supply of these workers). Employers may be less willing to employ or promote minority workers in this case. We would hypothesize that an increase in the unemployment rate for the preferred workers is expected to lower occupational opportunities for minority workers thereby increasing the difference in the occupational distributions of the two groups (i.e., $\tau_1 > 0$).

SUMMARY

The purpose of this chapter was to provide an empirically operational definition of a local labor market (the SMSA) and to describe how conditions in the market might influence discrimination against women and blacks. Furthermore, this chapter outlined a general model with which various hypotheses concerning the relationship between local market conditions and discrimination can be formulated and tested. The next chapter gives the empirical specification and results of the model used in this analysis.

IV

The Wage Model: Empirical Specification
and Results

INTRODUCTION

The discussion in the previous Chapter centered around the concept of a local labor market and the influence that changes in local market conditions may have on the relative economic status of minorities. In 1970, the overall black/white ratio of median income for year round full-time workers was 0.67, while in 1980 the same figure was 0.70. By comparison, the female to male income ratio was 0.59 in 1970, and 0.60 in 1980 (U.S. Bureau of the Census 1983a). These types of earnings differences (and the sources thereof) are the subject of analysis in this Chapter.

The purpose of this Chapter is threefold: (1) to test whether the SMSA is the appropriate definition of a labor market for the empirical analysis; (2) to analyze sources of the black-white and male-female wage differential; and (3) to investigate the possible relationship between changes in labor market conditions and sources of the race and gender wage differential. As mentioned in Chapter III, the notion of a labor market emphasized in this study is an SMSA.

DATA

An optimal data set that would be beneficial in formulating empirical models that explain variations in earnings and occupations among groups of workers should contain the following type of information: (1) numerous observations on individuals by specific SMSA's; (2) type and highest level of schooling attained by each individual (e.g., type of major, etc.); (3) specific information concerning an individual's job tenure and on-the-job training; (4) detailed information on other socioeconomic characteristics (e.g., the number and age of children, etc.); (5) information by employers on applicants for given jobs and those who were actually hired; and (6) detailed information concerning the SMSA. Although this list is not exhaustive, it indicates the nature of the requisite information needed to conduct such a labor market analysis. Unfortunately, such a comprehensive data set is currently not available. Hence, we face the same data constraints as other researchers in the area.

The data utilized in this study are drawn from the Public Use Samples of the 1970 and 1980 U.S. Census of Population and Housing. The comprehensiveness of the data coupled with the ability to draw relatively large samples from SMSA's are two reasons why the Census data are useful for the present analysis. Data sets such as the National Longitudinal Survey and the Panel Study of Income Dynamics, while providing comprehensive socioeconomic information, do not provide enough observations within each SMSA to conduct such detailed research of wage and occupational differentials.

The SMSA's used in this analysis were chosen from the largest 125 SMSA's, with a population of 250,000 or more in both 1970 and 1980, containing a representative cross section of white and black males and white females. To be included in this study, an SMSA had to have each of the three groups represented by a sample size of approximately 100 individuals or more from the 1-in-100 Public Use Sample. Using this criteria, 55 SMSA's were chosen.

Table 4.1 lists the 55 SMSA's and their respective states. Some SMSA's overlap state boundaries. For example, Cincinnati, Ohio also includes persons residing in neighboring portions of Kentucky and Indiana. The second column of Table 4.1 shows the primary state in which the SMSA is located, while the third column shows neighboring states whose residents are also included in that particular SMSA.

Two of the SMSA's used in this study were defined as an SMSA in 1970. One, Nassau-Suffolk County, NY, does not include a city, so for 1970 the two counties were combined and treated as an SMSA. The other, Dallas/Ft. Worth, consisted of two SMSA's in 1970. For the purpose of this study, the two were combined and treated as one SMSA in 1970. Overall, the labor force participants from the 55 SMSA's represented approximately 44 percent of the total civilian labor force in both 1970 and 1980 (Census 1983a, Table 247; Census 1973a, Table 3). For black males, 52.7 and 60.7 percent of the civilian black male labor force are represented by participants residing in the 55 SMSA's in 1970 and 1980 respectively.

Table 4.1 Sample of SMSA's		
SMSA Name	State	Also Includes Persons in Neighboring
Akron	OH	
Atlanta	GA	
Baltimore	MD	
Baton Rouge	LA	
Beaumont (Port Arthur-Orange)	TX	
Birmingham	AL	
Boston	MA	
Buffalo	NY	
Charleston (North Charleston)	SC	
Charlotte (Gastonia)	NC	
Chicago	IL	
Cincinnati	OH	KY,IN
Cleveland	OH	
Columbia	SC	
Columbus	OH	
Dallas/Ft. Worth	TX	
Dayton	OH	
Detroit	MI	
Flint	MI	
Ft. Lauderdale (Hollywood)	FL	
Gary (Hammond-East Chicago)	IN	
Greensboro (Winston-Salem,High Point)	NC	
Hartford	CT	
Houston	TX	
Indianapolis	IN	
Jackson	MS	
Jacksonville	FL	
Kansas City	MO	KA
Louisville	KY	IN
LA/Long Beach (Los Angeles)	CA	
Memphis	TN	AR,MS
Miami	FL	

Table 4.1 Sample of SMSA's		
SMSA Name	State	Also Includes Persons in Neighboring
Philadelphia	PA	NJ
Pittsburgh	PA	
Richmond	VA	
Rochester	NY	
St. Louis	MO	IL
San Antonio	TX	
San Diego	CA	
San Francisco (Oakland)	CA	
Shreveport	LA	
Tampa/St. Petersburg	FL	
Toledo	OH	MI
Washington D.C.		MD,VA
Wilmington	DE	NJ,MD

The sample of individuals residing in the 55 SMSA's is taken from the 1970 1-in-100 5% questionnaire and the 1980 1-in-100 Sample B file. The samples consist of white and black males, and white females, aged 18-64 who were non-students, and non-agricultural workers at the time the sample was taken. Information in the samples is based on U.S. Census data collected in 1970 and 1980. In both years individuals were asked questions concerning labor force participation (i.e., earnings, unemployment, hours worked, etc.), for the preceding calendar year. The information used in this study are based on self-reported responses by individuals.

In general, economic conditions for 1969 and 1979 were as follows: In 1969, real GNP grew 2.4 percent compared to 0.9 percent in 1979; the Consumer Price Index (CPI) rose 5.4 percent in 1969 compared with an increase of 11.3 percent in 1979; the unemployment rate remained in the 3.3 - 4.0 percent range in 1969, whereas it ranged between 5.7 and 5.9 percent in 1979; in 1969 the civilian labor force totaled 80,734,000 compared to 102,908,000 in 1979 (Economic Report of the President 1980, p. 205, p. 248, p. 250, p. 313).

WAGE MODELS

Empirical Specification. In examining the relative earnings of blacks and women under different labor market conditions, a model must be formulated that: (1) tests for the appropriate definition of a labor market (i.e., national versus local market) and (2) tests how the relative earnings position of women and blacks may be influenced by labor market conditions.

One approach in determining the above is to make use of the human capital earnings approach. The earnings models (equation 3-4) used in this dissertation are based upon the human capital model of income determination, developed by Mincer (1974), Chiswick (1974) and others. The dependent variable, (ln W) is the logarithm of annual earnings, measured as reported wage and salary income. The explanatory variables (X_1) include years of schooling (EDUCATION), years of potential labor market experience (EXPER = Age - EDUCATION - 5), years of labor market experience raised to higher ordered terms (see Murphy and Welch 1987), the logarithm of weeks worked (lnWW), and dummy variables for work limiting disability (DISAB), part-time work (PART), and self employment income (SELF).

The specified earnings model from above may, however, be subject to sample selection bias (see Heckman 1980). Selection bias will be a problem if unobservable factors that influence whether or not individuals are in the sample also influence wages. When estimating a wage equation, data are confined to a sample consisting of those individuals with an observed wage. This procedure will, thus, omit individuals whose reservation wages have not been met and hence, choose not to work (i.e., they are not in the labor force). Since wages are observed for only those individuals who work, the expected value of the observed wage (i.e., equation [3–4]) is:

(4–1) $E(\ln W | Xi, \text{in sample}) = X_1\beta + E(\epsilon_i | \text{in sample})$

If participation in the labor force is not random, then given X, the $E(\epsilon_i | \text{in sample}) \neq 0$ (Reimers 1983, p. 571). The error term in the wage equation, when treated as conditional on being employed (and in the sample), has a nonzero mean and may be correlated with exogenous variables in the wage equation (see Reimers 1983; Blau and Beller 1988; Shackett and Trapani 1987). Because of this, the average observed wage is subject to selectivity bias, as are the ordinary least squares estimates of the coefficients in the wage equation.

Heckman (1980) suggested a technique to obtain consistent estimates of the coefficients and standard errors in the wage equations. Following Heckman's model, we assume an individual works if the market wage (w_1) exceeds the individual's reservation wage (w^R_i). If Q_i = ln w_i - ln w^R_i, the individual will choose to participate in the labor market if $Q_i > 0$. The labor force participation decision of an individual (Q_i) is postulated to be a function of observables (Z_i) and a function of unobservable factors (u_i). The participation expression $(Q)_{,i}$ may be expressed as:

(4-2) $Q_i = Z_i \delta + u_i$

where $E(u_i) = 0$. Given expressions (4–1) and (4–2), Heckman shows

(4-3) $E(\epsilon_i|$ in sample$) = E(\epsilon_i|Q_i > o) = (\sigma_{u\epsilon} / \sigma_\epsilon)$ LAMBDA$_i$

where $\sigma_{u\epsilon}$ is the covariance between U and ϵ, σ_ϵ is the standard deviation of ϵ, and LAMBDA is the inverse of the Mills ratio[1] (see Heckman 1980, p. 214; Berger and Glenn 1986, p. 292). The inverse of the Mill's ratio (LAMBDA) is estimated from a probit model that predicts inclusion in the wage regression sample.

Heckman further suggests that selection bias may be corrected by entering the estimates of LAMBDA$_i$ as a regressor in the wage equation (3–4). For each race/sex group the expanded wage equation to be estimated becomes:

(4-4)   ln $W_i = X_i\beta + b$ LAMBDA$_i + \mu_i$

where b is the parameter ($\sigma_{u\epsilon} / \sigma_\epsilon$) to be estimated and μ is an error term distributed with zero mean but is heteroscedastic (Heckman 1980, pp. 215–216). Estimating β from ordinary least squares does, however, provide consistent and efficient estimates under a null hypothesis of no selection bias (Heckman 1980, p. 216; Berger and Glenn 1986, p. 292).

To correct for possible sample selection bias, we again adopt Heckman's (1980) procedure. That is, for each race/sex group the participation equation (4–2) is specified such that $Q = 1$ if the individual worked, and $Q = 0$ otherwise. The participation equation is estimated using a probit model of qualitative choice. The probit model assumes that the variable Q_i is a random variable with a normal distribution. This allows the probability of Q_i to be calculated from the cumulative normal probability function (see Pindyk and Rubinfeld 1981, pp. 281–283). The estimates of the probit model yield the probability P_1, which is an estimate that an individual will participate in the labor force given their characteristics Z_i.

Included in the probit participation equations are the variables: years of education and its square, potential labor market experience (also raised to higher order terms), marital status, presence of health problems that limit or prevent labor market work, and for women, the number of children (see Table 4.2 for a description of the variables). Also included is a variable indicating whether or not the individual is 62 years of age or older. This variable attempts to measure whether an individual is eligible for benefits, such as Social Security, which may limit that individual's labor force participation (Blau and Beller 1988, p. 517). The specification of the probit equation is similar to that employed by other researchers (see Berger and Glenn 1986; Reimers 1983; Blau and Beller 1988 as a few examples). Thus, the parameters of the wage model specified in equation (4–4) are estimated using ordinary least squares estimation procedures as modified by Heckman and others.

The wage structures (4–4) are estimated using those individuals who reported positive wage and salary income and positive weeks worked for 1969 and 1979. For those individuals who reported nonzero self-employment income (in addition to wage and salary income), a dummy variable (SELF = 1) is included. Table 4.3 gives a complete list of the variables used to estimate the wage structure (4–4) for each race/sex group.

Table 4.2
Variable Definitions for the Participation Equation

1.	Q_i	=	1 if the individual worked (i.e., participated in the labor force
		=	0 otherwise
2.	EDUCATION	=	Years of schooling completed by the individual
3.	EXPER	=	estimated years of experience for each individual (calculated as AGE - EDUCATION - 5)
4.	DISABILITY	=	1 if individual reports that a disability limits or prohibits labor force participation
		=	0 otherwise
5.	MSP	=	1 if individual is married with spouse present
		=	0 otherwise
6.	AGE62	=	1 if the individual is 62 years of age or older
		=	0 otherwise
7.	KIDS	=	for women, the number of children ever born

Using the wage model (4–4), a test may be formulated which suggests the appropriate definition of a labor market (i.e., a national market or a local market). Multivariate regression techniques are used to estimate the parameters contained in equation (4–4) for black men, white women, and white men based on a pooled sample from the 55 SMSA's. A national labor market (represented by the pooled regression) constrains the coefficients to be equal across cities. The sample of J (55) SMSA's is taken to depict the various local labor markets. For each of the 55 SMSA's an earnings equation (containing the same variables) is estimated for each of the three groups. Thus, for each of the groups, the following equations exist:

(4–5) $\ln W'^{natl}_i = x_i \beta'^{natl} + b'^{natl} LAMBDA^{natl}_i + e'^{natl}_i$
         for, $i = 1, \ldots, n$

Table 4.3
Variable Definitions for the Wage Equation

1. EARNINGS =	Annual wage and salary earnings for each observation.
2. EDUCATION =	Years of schooling completed by the individual.
3. EXPER =	estimated years of experience for each individual (calculated as AGE - EDUCATION - 5)
4. DISABILITY =	1 if individual reports that a disability limits labor force participation
=	0 otherwise
5. LN WEEKS WORKED =	the logrithim of the number of weeks the individual worked
6. PART =	1 if individual worked part time (i.e., if the individual usually worked 35 hours or less a week)
=	0 otherwise
7. SELF =	1 if the individual reported nonfarm self employment income (or loss in addition to wage and salary income
=	0 otherwise
8. LAMBDA =	Inverse of Mill's ration predicted from a probit equation for inclusion in the wage sample

(4–6) $\ln W_i^{'j} = X_i \beta^{'j} + b^{'j} \, LAMBDA_i^j + e_i^{'j}$
for $i = 1, \ldots, r;\ \ j = 1, \ldots, J$

where equation (4–5) represents the estimated earnings equation based on the pooled sample, equation (4–6) represents each of the J estimated earnings equations (for each SMSA), X is the vector of explanatory variables, LAMBDA is the inverse of the Mill's ratio, β' is a vector of the estimated regression coefficients, e_i' is a vector of the residuals, r is the number of observations in each SMSA, and n is the number of observations in the national sample (where $n = \Sigma_j r$). The null hypothesis is:

(4–7) $H_o : \beta^1 = \beta^2 = \ldots = \beta^J = \beta^{natl}$

(i.e, whether or not the coefficients vary across SMSA's).   The
appropriate test is given by (see Johnston 1984, pp. 414–415):

$$F = [(SSE^{natl} - SSE^{SMSA})/k(J - 1)] / [SSE^{SMSA}/(n - Jk)]$$

where SSE^{natl} is the residual sum of squares from equation (4–5),
         SSE^{SMSA} is the sum of the residual sum of squares for the J
         equations $[= \Sigma_j (e'^j_j 'e'^j_i)]$,
         J is the number of SMSAs,
         k is the number of estimated coefficients in each equation
         r is the number of observations in the jth SMSA.
         N is the total sample size (which equals $\Sigma_j r$).

Under the null hypothesis, the above is distributed as F with [k(J - 1), n -
Jk] degrees of freedom. Rejection of the null hypothesis would indicate
that the coefficients contained in the human capital earnings equations
vary across SMSAs and signals that wage structures differ across labor
markets. This would then imply the U.S. may not generally be viewed as
an aggregate labor market.

Empirical Results: Wage Models. Tables 4.4 and 4.5 show the estimated
coefficients for the pooled regression (i.e., equation 4–5) for 1970 and
1980. In the white male equations, education, experience, and weeks
worked have positive coefficients, whereas part-time status and self-
employment income have negative coefficients. In the 1980 black male
equation, the signs on the coefficients are the same as those for white
men. However, for black men in 1970 and for white women in both years,
the coefficient on education has a negative sign, although the sign on the
squared term is positive in all cases. In 1970, the full effect of education
is positive for all black men with one or more years of schooling and for
white women with nine or more years of schooling. In 1980, education
is associated with higher earnings for women with 4 or more years of
schooling. This suggests that, in general, the overall effect of education

Table 4.4 Estimated Earnings Equations: 1970 Sample Dependent Variable: Logarithm of Annual Earnings (Standard Errors in Parentheses)			
Exogenous Variable	White Men	Black Men	White Women
Constant	3.31480 (0.02534	4.03271 (0.06612)	2.90735 (0.02779)
EDUCATION	0.01259 (0.00220	-0.00256 (0.00552)	-0.04595 (0.00353)
EDUC2	0.00252 (0.00009)	0.00271 (0.00028)	0.00513 (0.00015)
EXPER	0.11516 (0.00218)	0.08402 (0.00665)	0.09316 (0.00333)
EXPER2	-0.00480 (0.00016)	-0.00373 (0.00047)	-0.00629 (0.00025)
EXPER3	0.00008 (0.00000)	0.00007 (0.00001)	0.00016 (0.000007)
EXPER4	-4.82e-07 (4.33e-08)	-4.66e-07 (1.15e-07)	-0.000001 (6.65e-08)
PART-TIME	-0.10506 (0.00432)	-0.14795 (0.01139)	-0.32255 (0.00485)
SELF-EMPLOY	-0.06969 (0.00744)	-0.04808 (0.03556)	-0.14201 (0.01911)
lnWW	1.12483 (0.00565)	0.97311 (0.01386	1.31184 (0.00445)
DISABILITY	0.21004 (0.00965	0.39957 (0.31692)	0.04538 (0.01013)

Table 4.4
Estimated Earnings Equations: 1970 Pooled Sample
Dependent Variable: Logarithm of Annual Earnings (Standard
Errors in Parentheses)

Exogenous Variable	White Men	Black Men	White Women
LAMBDA	-1.51738 (0.03515)	-1.53041 (0.08307)	-0.35161 (0.01516)
R^2	.4509	.3522	.5782
SSE	54123.65892	11582.71376	57872.28328
n	157929	24026	112706

Table 4.5
Estimated Earnings Equations: 1980 Pooled Sample
Dependent Variable: Logarithm of Annual Earnings
(Standard Errors in Parentheses)

Exogenous Variable	White Men	Black Men	White Women
Constant	4.424334 (0.02403)	4.8839996 (0.06537)	4.23094 (0.02526)
EDUCATION	0.05645 (0.00246)	0.01226 (0.00652	-0.01496 (0.00327)
EDUC2	0.00053 (0.00009)	0.00159 (0.00028)	0.00341 (0.00013)
EXPER	0.08682 (0.00226)	0.08599 (0.00663)	0.09787 (0.00265)

Table 4.5 Estimated Earnings Equations: 1980 Pooled Sample Dependent Variable: Logarithm of Annual Earnings (Standard Errors in Parentheses)			
Exogenous Variable	White Men	Black Men	White Women
EXPER2	-0.00257 (0.00018)	-0.00374 (0.00049)	-0.00603 (0.00021)
EXPER3	0.00002 (0.000005)	0.00007 (0.00001)	0.00015 (0.000006)
EXPER4	1.07E-07 (5.26E-08)	-3.89E-07 (1.31E-07)	-0.000001 (6.27E-08)
PART-TIME	-0.49965 (0.00698)	-0.40652 (0.01593)	-0.72538 (0.00428)
SELF-EMPLOY	-0.18909 (0.00772)	-0.15813 (0.03833)	-0.23322 (0.01511)
lnWW	1.01283 (0.00432)	0.96268 (0.00918)	1.07480 (0.00294)
DISABILITY	0.23433 (0.01444)	0.53031 (0.04298)	0.00279 (0.01154)
LAMBDA	-1.37781 (0.04038)	-1.78088 (0.09751)	-0.52835 (0.02099)
R^2	.4716	.4590	.6506
SSE	67426.8802	15722.7067	54283.6619
n	168253	27266	132023

on earnings is positive. The signs of the estimated coefficients of these variables are consistent with the findings of other researchers (see Oaxaca 1973a, 1973b; Gwartney and Long 1978; Carlson and Swartz 1988, as a few examples).

For all three groups in both years, the coefficient on LAMBDA (used to correct for selectivity bias) is negative. This means that unobservables that positively affect the probability of working, negatively affect wage and salary earnings. The negative coefficient suggests that those individuals who were in the wage and salary sector earned less, holding the measured characteristics constant, than those outside the wage and salary sector. This implies that individuals outside the wage and salary sector might have better opportunities elsewhere, and hence, are less likely to be included in the wage sample. Workers who are not employed in the wage and salary sector (and are, therefore, not included in our sample) may instead be in the military, totally self-employed, engaged in home production, involved in illegal market activity , or out of the paid labor force. This result has been supported by Reimers (1983) and Blau and Ferber (1988) for men.

Similarly, the wage structure (4–4) for each race/sex group is estimated separately for each SMSA for both 1970 and 1980.

In testing hypothesis (4–7), the results of the estimated wage equations for both the pooled (i.e., national) sample and the individual SMSA's are used to calculate the appropriate test statistic. Table 4.6 summarizes the test statistics for each group in each year. The calculated F-statistics reported in Table 4.6 indicate that the null hypothesis is rejected in all instances. This suggests that the wage structures of white men, black men, and white women differ across SMSA's. Given these results, the use of the local labor market (SMSA) appears appropriate in this analysis.

WAGE DECOMPOSITION MODEL

From the previous hypothesis test, it was determined that a local labor market (approximated by the SMSA) is preferred to a national labor market in this analysis. The SMSA is used to analyze the possible impact that labor market conditions have on earnings differentials among different groups of workers. This section compares earnings among groups of workers and assesses the degree to which differences in socioeconomic traits between groups of workers account for possible race and gender earnings differentials. This analysis employs wage decomposition methods developed by Blinder (1973) and Oaxaca (1973a, 1973b) along with further extensions developed by Reimers (1983).

Table 4.6
Hypotheses and Test Statistics for Testing a National vs. Local Labor Market

Hypothesis (4-7)
$$H_o : \beta^1 = \beta^2 = \ldots = \beta^{55} = \beta^{natl}$$
$$H_a : \beta\text{'s are not equal}$$

Group	Test Statistic (F-Statistic)	
	1970	1980
White Males	9.373[a]	7.315[a]
Black Males	2.967[a]	2.152[a]
White Females	7.896[a]	10.129[a]

[a]H_o rejected at 1% level of significance.

Empirical Specification. This application of the wage decomposition method utilizes the earnings equations that have been estimated for each SMSA for the years 1970 and 1980. Employing the Blinder/Oaxaca method, the gross average earnings differential between two groups of workers (A and B) in each SMSA may be defined as:

$$(4\text{-}8) \quad G = \overline{\ln W_a} - \overline{\ln W_b}$$

G may further be expressed in terms of the estimated form of the wage model (4-6):

$$(4\text{-}9) \quad G = [\overline{X_a}\beta'_a + b'_a \overline{LAMBDA_a}] - [\overline{X_b}\beta'_b + b'_b \overline{LAMBDA_b}]$$

where the prime (') notation denotes estimated parameters and the bar (-) notation indicates that the explanatory variables are evaluated at their sample mean values.

Assuming that workers from group B encounter the wage structure from workers in group A in the absence of earnings discrimination, G may be rewritten as [2]:

$$(4-10) \quad G = [(\overline{X}_a - \overline{X}_b)\beta'_a] + [\overline{X}_b(\beta'_a - \beta'_b)] + [b'_a \overline{LAMBDA_a} - b'_b \overline{LAMBDA_b}]$$

The gross average earnings differential (G) is now composed of three parts (Reimers 1983; p. 572):

    i.   that due to differences in average characteristics of the two groups;

    ii.   that due to differences in the parameters of the wage function;

    iii.   that due to differences in selectivity bias.

Reimers (1983) suggests further modification of the earnings differential, G, which allows us to calculate a wage differential between two groups of workers that is corrected for selectivity bias. According to Reimers, this difference incorporates wage possibilities of workers both in, and outside the wage and salary sector (p. 572). The corrected wage difference is expressed as:

$$(4-11) \quad \overline{lnW_a} - \overline{lnW_b} - [b'_a \overline{LAMBDA_a} - b'_b \overline{LAMBDA_b}]$$

which is equivalent to,

$$(4-12) \quad [(\overline{X}_a - \overline{X}_b)\beta'_a] + [\overline{X}_b(\beta'_a - \beta'_b)].$$

The first bracketed term in equation (4–12) represents what is generally interpreted as an estimate of the nondiscriminatory portion (the so-called endowment effect) of the earnings differential; while the second bracketed term represents the residual component — what analysts frequently attribute as an upper bound estimate of wage discrimination) (see Blinder 1973; Oaxaca 1973; Chiplin 1974).[3]

Using this approach, the earnings differential (and sources thereof) for black men and white women can be calculated using white males as the reference group. The following section presents the empirical results of the wage decomposition model based on the specification in equation (4-12), for each race and gender group by SMSA in 1970 and 1980.

Empirical Results: Wage Decomposition. Earnings decomposition of the estimated earnings equation (4–12) are calculated for black men and white women for each SMSA in both 1970 and 1980. The results of these calculations are presented in tables 4.7, 4.8, 4.9, and 4.10.

In each of the tables, column 1 corresponds to the observed log wage difference between the minority group (group B) and white males (group A). The observed earnings difference is calculated as the difference in the mean log earnings of the two groups.

Column 2 of tables 4.7 through 4.10 corresponds to the earnings difference between the minority group and white men, having corrected for sample selection bias. This term corresponds to equation (4–11). If white men have a larger negative selectivity bias than the corresponding minority group, the selectivity bias correction will widen the earnings differential between the two groups. This implies that the "wage offer" differential is larger than the observed wage differential (see Reimers 1983, p. 574). The corrected wage gap may widen if minority workers who possess lower skills (and hence, lower expected wages) drop out of the labor force in favor of non-market activities (see Butler and Heckman 1977 and Brown 1984). This issue will be discussed further below.

Column 3 of each table corresponds to the earnings difference that cannot be explained by differences in observed productivity-related characteristics. As mentioned above, this difference, due to differences in earnings equation parameters, is what researchers frequently attribute to discrimination (Blinder 1973; Oaxaca 1973a, 1973b). Column 4 expresses this unexplained portion as a percent of the selectivity corrected earnings difference between the two groups.[4] The last two columns in the tables gives the sample size of the reference group (white males) and the minority group. Also, the last entry in each table gives an estimate of the above items for the United States as a whole. These national estimates, calculated for comparative purposes, are based on the 1-1000 Public Use Samples from 1970 and 1980. Included in this cross-sectional sample are individuals from the entire United States (and not just the 55 SMSA's).

Table 4.7
1970 Black/White Male Earnings Difference by SMSA

SMSA	(1) Average Earnings Difference[a] (in logs)	(2) Earnings Difference Corrected for Selectivity Bias[b]	(3) Unexplained Earnings Difference[c] (in logs)	(4) Percent of Corrected Earnings Difference Unexplained[d]	Sample Size White	Sample Size Black
Akron	0.593	0.654	0.454	69.473	1395	99
Atlanta	0.643	0.475	0.200	42.124	2429	601
Baltimore	0.566	0.489	0.276	56.416	3457	893
BatonRouge	0.735	0.828	0.657	79.443	410	127
Beaumont	0.647	0.708	0.553	78.103	526	123
Birmingham	0.542	0.550	0.340	61.871	1109	348
Boston	0.421	0.365	0.204	55.903	7204	224
Buffalo	0.460	0.309	0.144	46.481	2640	200
Charleston	0.696	0.597	0.441	73.758	351	128
Charlotte	0.724	0.813	0.481	59.146	692	191

Table 4.7
1970 Black/White Male Earnings Difference by SMSA

SMSA	(1) Average Earnings Difference[a] (in logs)	(2) Earnings Difference Corrected for Selectivity Bias[b]	(3) Unexplained Earnings Difference[c] (in logs)	(4) Percent of Corrected Earnings Difference Unexplained[d]	Sample Size White	Sample Size Black
Chicago	0.442	0.403	0.237	58.813	12848	2183
Cincinnati	0.438	0.495	0.381	76.929	2537	263
Cleveland	0.463	0.350	0.211	60.260	3931	613
Columbia	0.653	0.708	0.412	58.236	443	119
Columbus	0.394	0.456	0.294	64.428	1626	184
Dallas/Ft. Worth	0.672	0.597	0.346	57.878	4417	591
Dayton	0.288	0.435	0.295	67.858	1652	162
Detroit	0.421	0.346	0.173	50.133	7620	1499
Flint	0.355	0.384	0.213	55.569	951	123
Ft.Lauderdale	0.713	0.693	0.505	72.811	1007	128

Table 4.7
1970 Black/White Male Earnings Difference by SMSA

SMSA	(1) Average Earnings Difference[a] (in logs)	(2) Earnings Difference Corrected for Selectivity Bias[b]	(3) Unexplained Earnings Difference[c] (in logs)	(4) Percent of Corrected Earnings Difference Unexplained[d]	Sample Size White	Sample Size Black
Gary	0.309	0.361	0.262	72.714	1209	199
Greensboro	0.596	0.478	0.264	55.310	1098	204
Hartford	0.424	0.519	0.418	80.511	1729	111
Houston	0.655	0.581	0.348	59.876	3659	695
Indianapolis	0.428	0.510	0.418	82.074	2129	258
Jackson	0.934	0.786	0.395	50.205	308	127
Jacksonville	0.577	0.417	0.198	47.476	818	172
KansasCity	0.377	0.333	0.213	63.974	2404	260
Louisville	0.563	0.598	0.502	83.966	1565	168
LA/LongBeach	0.422	0.431	0.291	67.446	13144	1369

62

Table 4.7
1970 Black/White Male Earnings Difference by SMSA

SMSA	(1) Average Earnings Difference[a] (in logs)	(2) Earnings Difference Corrected for Selectivity Bias[b]	(3) Unexplained Earnings Difference[c] (in logs)	(4) Percent of Corrected Earnings Difference Unexplained[d]	Sample Size White	Sample Size Black
Memphis	0.738	0.764	0.462	60.427	1012	409
Miami	0.528	0.590	0.412	69.762	2146	335
Milwaukee	0.477	0.425	0.209	49.071	2816	185
Mobile	0.664	0.642	0.331	51.581	539	169
Nashville	0.520	0.419	0.322	76.728	973	159
Nassau/Suffolk	0.651	0.811	0.599	73.839	6074	187
NewOrleans	0.690	0.523	0.367	70.154	1510	508
NewportNews	0.765	0.536	0.214	39.889	423	113
NewYork	0.369	0.260	0.121	46.506	15381	3120
Newark	0.512	0.413	0.159	38.405	3325	649

Table 4.7
1970 Black/White Male Earnings Difference by SMSA

SMSA	(1) Average Earnings Difference[a] (in logs)	(2) Earnings Difference Corrected for Selectivity Bias[b]	(3) Unexplained Earnings Difference[c] (in logs)	(4) Percent of Corrected Earnings Difference Unexplained[d]	Sample Size White	Sample Size Black
Norfolk	0.574	0.537	0.376	69.939	834	283
Orlando	0.787	1.008	0.732	72.636	728	94
Philadelphia	0.484	0.335	0.161	48.014	6565	1410
Pittsburgh	0.370	0.251	0.081	32.245	4892	278
Richmond	0.598	0.670	0.355	52.928	886	239
Rochester	0.616	0.652	0.376	57.701	1733	111
St.Louis	0.576	0.449	0.288	64.002	4250	584
SanAntonio	0.436	0.512	0.362	70.589	1313	92
SanDiego	0.351	0.362	0.085	23.600	2076	82
SanFrancisco	0.424	0.335	0.158	47.039	5725	606

64

Table 4.7
1970 Black/White Male Earnings Difference by SMSA

SMSA	(1) Average Earnings Difference[a] (in logs)	(2) Earnings Difference Corrected for Selectivity Bias[b]	(3) Unexplained Earnings Difference[c] (in logs)	(4) Percent of Corrected Earnings Difference Unexplained[d]	Sample Size White	Sample Size Black
Shreveport	0.815	0.708	0.496	70.154	380	142
Tampa/St.Pete	0.532	0.558	0.373	66.890	1502	182
Toledo	0.553	0.587	0.360	61.396	1346	100
WashingtonDC	0.622	0.581	0.292	50.270	4393	1372
Wilmington	0.562	0.662	0.488	73.635	965	106
UnitedStates	0.539	0.455	0.255	56.050	35317	3656

a $\overline{lnW}_a - \overline{lnW}_b$

b $\overline{lnW}_a - \overline{lnW}_b - [b'_a\overline{LAMBDA}_a - b'_b\overline{LAMBDA}_b]$

c $[\overline{X}_b(\beta'_a - \beta'_b)]$

d $\{[\overline{X}_b(\beta'_a - \beta'_b)] / [\overline{lnW}_a - \overline{lnW}_b - (b'_a\overline{LAMBDA}_a - b'_b\overline{LAMBDA}_b)]\}*100$

Table 4.8
1980 Black/White Male Earnings Difference by SMSA

SMSA	(1) Average Earnings Difference[a] (in logs)	(2) Earnings Difference Corrected for Selectivity Bias[b]	(3) Unexplained Earnings Difference[c] (in logs)	(4) Percent of Corrected Earnings Difference Unexplained[d]	Sample Size White	Sample Size Black
Akron	0.545	0.149	-0.122	-81.284	1419	103
Atlanta	0.578	0.270	-0.008	-2.934	3626	887
Baltimore	0.513	0.459	0.715	38.267	3752	958
BatonRouge	0.514	0.284	-0.018	-6.237	834	228
Beaumont	0.478	0.072	-0.152	-210.400	721	146
Birmingham	0.609	0.353	0.099	28.010	1397	388
Boston	0.469	0.560	0.364	64.905	5560	240
Buffalo	0.235	0.261	0.197	75.667	2458	240
Charleston	0.593	0.362	0.163	45.092	595	200
Charlotte	0.549	0.645	0.421	65.303	1200	252

Table 4.8

1980 Black/White Male Earnings Difference by SMSA

SMSA	(1) Average Earnings Difference[a] (in logs)	(2) Earnings Difference Corrected for Selectivity Bias[b]	(3) Unexplained Earnings Difference[c] (in logs)	(4) Percent of Corrected Earnings Difference Unexplained[d]	Sample Size White	Sample Size Black
Chicago	0.495	0.208	0.004	2.028	12704	2254
Cincinnati	0.562	0.317	0.283	47.188	2565	309
Cleveland	0.503	0.221	-0.018	-8.084	3671	580
Columbia	0.572	0.815	0.566	69.489	611	207
Columbus	0.383	0.424	0.247	58.149	2150	226
Dallas/Ft. Worth	0.574	0.397	0.168	42.297	5790	769
Dayton	0.487	0.321	0.166	51.772	1552	158
Detroit	0.514	0.323	0.046	14.305	8070	1505
Flint	0.123	0.231	0.142	61.326	997	134
Ft.Lauderdale	0.603	0.498	0.301	60.458	1776	193

67

Table 4.8
1980 Black/White Male Earnings Difference by SMSA

SMSA	(1) Average Earnings Difference[a] (in logs)	(2) Earnings Difference Corrected for Selectivity Bias[b]	(3) Unexplained Earnings Difference[c] (in logs)	(4) Percent of Corrected Earnings Difference Unexplained[d]	Sample Size White	Sample Size Black
Gary	0.306	0.207	0.061	29.588	1262	227
Greensboro	0.386	0.431	0.276	64.110	1389	254
Hartford	0.402	0.394	0.238	60.344	1530	110
Houston	0.516	0.289	0.103	35.500	5622	1043
Indianapolis	0.596	0.491	0.119	24.291	2391	296
Jackson	0.707	0.823	0.578	70.290	462	179
Jacksonville	0.501	0.382	0.113	38.430	2655	296
KansasCity	0.346	0.294	0.186	53.592	1854	187
Louisville	0.396	0.347	0.186	53.592	1854	187
LA/LongBeach	0.402	0.292	0.136	46.458	11603	1644

Table 4.8
1980 Black/White Male Earnings Difference by SMSA

SMSA	(1) Average Earnings Difference[a] (in logs)	(2) Earnings Difference Corrected for Selectivity Bias[b]	(3) Unexplained Earnings Difference[c] (in logs)	(4) Percent of Corrected Earnings Difference Unexplained[d]	Sample Size White	Sample Size Black
Memphis	0.672	0.490	0.196	40.025	1064	519
Miami	0.526	0.305	0.017	5.560	2543	490
Milwaukee	0.489	0.386	0.167	43.287	1988	245
Mobile	0.499	0.690	0.483	70.075	712	208
Nashville	0.429	0.344	0.231	67.124	1615	241
Nassau/Suffolk	0.312	0.296	0.211	71.102	5454	274
New Orleans	0.659	0.577	0.329	57.109	1834	591
NewportNews	0.535	0.509	0.317	62.333	520	184
New York	0.465	0.357	0.163	45.482	13515	3091
Newark	0.509	0.412	0.202	48.888	3566	728

Table 4.8
1980 Black/White Male Earnings Difference by SMSA

SMSA	(1) Average Earnings Difference[a] (in logs)	(2) Earnings Difference Corrected for Selectivity Bias[b]	(3) Unexplained Earnings Difference[c] (in logs)	(4) Percent of Corrected Earnings Difference Unexplained[d]	Sample Size White	Sample Size Black
Norfolk	0.479	0.478	0.161	33.787	787	254
Orlando	0.592	0.701	0.419	59.776	1314	127
Philadelphia	0.481	0.248	0.035	14.209	8248	1356
Pittsburgh	0.444	0.407	0.178	43.665	4743	265
Richmond	0.497	0.512	0.231	45.099	1120	344
Rochester	0.544	0.537	0.156	29.039	2012	125
St.Louis	0.531	0.302	0.105	34.632	4471	620
SanAntonio	0.360	0.468	0.270	57.800	1612	114
SanDiego	0.560	0.606	0.256	42.228	2893	145
SanFrancisco	0.440	0.419	0.240	57.144	5480	692

Table 4.8
1980 Black/White Male Earnings Difference by SMSA

SMSA	(1) Average Earnings Difference[a] (in logs)	(2) Earnings Difference Corrected for Selectivity Bias[b]	(3) Unexplained Earnings Difference[c] (in logs)	(4) Percent of Corrected Earnings Difference Unexplained[d]	Sample Size White	Sample Size Black
Shreveport	0.656	0.175	-0.116	-66.073	535	169
Tampa/St.Pete	0.398	0.346	0.178	51.597	2483	241
Toledo	0.375	0.382	0.236	61.804	1622	116
WashingtonD.C.	0.545	0.377	0.069	18.357	4910	1642
Wilmington	0.548	0.414	0.175	42.170	806	118
UnitedStates	0.487	0.340	0.107	31.575	40357	4250

a $\overline{lnW_a} - \overline{lnW_b}$

b $\overline{lnW_a} - \overline{lnW_b} - [b'_a\overline{LAMBDA_a} - b'_b\overline{LAMBDA_b}]$

c $[\overline{X_b}(\beta'_a - \beta'_b)]$

d $\{[\overline{X_b}(\beta'_a - \beta'_b)] / [\overline{lnW_a} - \overline{lnW_b} - (b'_a\overline{LAMBDA_a} - b'_b\overline{LAMBDA_b})]\}*100$

Table 4.9
1970 White Male/White Female Earnings Difference by SMSA

SMSA	(1) Observed Average Earnings Difference[a] (in logs)	(2) Earnings Difference Corrected for Selectivity Bias[b]	(3) Unexplained Earnings Difference[c] (in logs)	(4) Percent of Corrected Earnings Difference Unexplained[d]	Sample Size Men	Sample Size Women
Akron	1.207	1.204	0.762	63.288	1395	877
Atlanta	1.002	0.977	0.515	52.743	2429	1905
Baltimore	0.970	1.117	0.749	67.049	3457	2411
BatonRouge	1.086	1.167	0.800	68.555	410	253
Beaumont	1.246	1.439	0.930	64.604	526	279
Birmingham	1.039	1.061	0.717	67.493	1109	761
Boston	1.015	0.974	0.577	59.255	7204	5737
Buffalo	1.142	1.112	0.759	68.199	2640	1726
Charleston	1.139	1.169	0.566	59.245	351	286
Charlotte	0.997	0.986	0.693	57.373	692	562

72

Table 4.9
1970 White Male/White Female Earnings Difference by SMSA

SMSA	(1) Observed Average Earnings Difference[a] (in logs)	(2) Earnings Difference Corrected for Selectivity Bias[b]	(3) Unexplained Earnings Difference[c] (in logs)	(4) Percent of Corrected Earnings Difference Unexplained[d]	Sample Size Men	Sample Size Women
Chicago	1.044	0.976	0.577	59.109	12848	8965
Cincinnati	1.112	1.105	0.702	63.515	2537	1696
Cleveland	1.096	0.967	0.590	61.031	3931	2601
Columbia	0.859	0.727	0.409	56.317	443	359
Columbus	1.058	1.023	0.605	59.132	1626	1270
Dallas/Ft. Worth	1.068	1.009	0.555	55.038	4417	3329
Dayton	1.170	1.064	0.618	58.133	1652	1085
Detroit	1.120	1.075	0.668	62.154	7620	4664
Flint	1.241	1.267	0.771	60.890	951	570
Ft.Lauderdale	1.075	1.202	0.819	68.097	1007	816

Table 4.9
1970 White Male/White Female Earnings Difference by SMSA

SMSA	(1) Observed Average Earnings Difference[a] (in logs)	(2) Earnings Difference Corrected for Selectivity Bias[b]	(3) Unexplained Earnings Difference[c] (in logs)	(4) Percent of Corrected Earnings Difference Unexplained[d]	Sample Size Men	Sample Size Women
Gary	1.301	1.260	0.884	70.167	1209	631
Greensboro	0.826	0.781	0.390	49.902	1098	915
Hartford	0.981	0.840	0.537	63.972	1729	1295
Houston	1.096	1.135	0.655	57.653	3659	2412
Indianapolis	1.085	1.006	0.657	65.347	2129	1575
Jackson	1.140	1.107	0.513	46.315	308	269
Jacksonville	0.994	0.828	0.466	56.336	818	628
KansasCity	1.019	0.951	0.512	53.888	2404	1901
Louisville	1.028	1.194	0.815	68.258	1565	1105
LA/LongBeach	0.922	0.936	0.569	60.778	13144	9623

Table 4.9
1970 White Male/White Female Earnings Difference by SMSA

SMSA	(1) Observed Average Earnings Difference[a] (in logs)	(2) Earnings Difference Corrected for Selectivity Bias[b]	(3) Unexplained Earnings Difference[c] (in logs)	(4) Percent of Corrected Earnings Difference Unexplained[d]	Sample Size Men	Sample Size Women
Memphis	1.072	1.009	0.511	50.685	1012	798
Miami	0.886	0.925	0.643	69.475	2146	1771
Milwaukee	1.198	1.206	0.791	65.635	2816	2090
Mobile	1.105	0.870	0.360	41.436	539	347
Nashville	0.859	0.953	0.569	59.693	973	799
Nassau/Suffolk	1.246	1.196	0.711	59.437	5074	3155
NewOrleans	0.921	0.900	0.568	63.115	1510	1016
NewportNews	1.123	0.922	0.333	36.087	423	327
NewYork	0.689	0.704	0.456	64.812	15381	11464
Newark	1.071	0.988	0.617	62.444	3325	2278

75

Table 4.9
1970 White Male/White Female Earnings Difference by SMSA

SMSA	(1) Observed Average Earnings Difference[a] (in logs)	(2) Earnings Difference Corrected for Selectivity Bias[b]	(3) Unexplained Earnings Difference[c] (in logs)	(4) Percent of Corrected Earnings Difference Unexplained[d]	Sample Size Men	Sample Size Women
Norfolk	1.100	0.940	0.444	47.298	834	680
Orlando	1.066	1.244	0.804	64.582	728	546
Philadelphia	1.011	1.003	0.638	63.645	6565	4588
Pittsburgh	1.103	1.020	0.617	60.478	4892	2814
Richmond	0.933	0.941	0.535	56.850	886	687
Rochester	1.123	1.051	0.646	61.398	1733	1258
St.Louis	1.134	1.091	0.696	63.735	4250	2950
SanAntonio	0.934	0.930	0.443	47.654	1313	1019
SanDiego	1.119	1.122	0.624	55.588	2076	1648
SanFrancisco	0.920	0.923	0.538	58.298	5725	4181

Table 4.9
1970 White Male/White Female Earnings Difference by SMSA

SMSA	(1) Observed Average Earnings Difference[a] (in logs)	(2) Earnings Difference Corrected for Selectivity Bias[b]	(3) Unexplained Earnings Difference[c] (in logs)	(4) Percent of Corrected Earnings Difference Unexplained[d]	Sample Size Men	Sample Size Women
Shreveport	1.048	0.892	0.529	59.222	380	271
Tampa/St.Pete	1.013	1.040	0.615	59.149	1502	1233
Toledo	1.177	1.143	0.763	66.772	1346	905
WashingtonD.C.	0.989	0.881	0.409	46.386	4393	3577
Wilmington	1.141	1.156	0.768	66.445	965	598
UnitedStates	1.052	1.015	0.623	61.428	35317	25819

$a \quad \overline{lnW_a} - \overline{lnW_b}$

$b \quad \overline{lnW_a} - \overline{lnW_b} - [\overline{b'_a LAMBDA} - \overline{b'_b LAMBDA_b}]$

$c \quad [\overline{X_b(\beta'_b)}]$

$d \quad \{[\overline{X_b(\beta'_a} - \beta'_b)] / [\overline{lnW_a} - \overline{lnW_b} - (\overline{b'_a LAMBDA_a} - \overline{b'_b LAMBDA_b})]\}*100$

77

Table 4.10
1980 White Male/White Female Earnings Difference by SMSA

SMSA	(1) Average Earnings Difference[a] (in logs)	(2) Earnings Difference Corrected for Selectivity Bias[b]	(3) Unexplained Earnings Difference[c] (in logs)	(4) Percent of Corrected Earnings Difference Unexplained[d]	Sample Size Men	Sample Size Women
Akron	1.071	1.019	0.687	67.404	1419	987
Atlanta	0.852	0.846	0.502	59.398	3626	3039
Baltimore	0.891	0.897	0.516	57.512	3752	2855
BatonRouge	0.984	1.036	0.611	58.916	834	545
Beaumont	1.322	1.181	0.711	60.230	721	418
Birmingham	0.939	0.841	0.443	52.628	1397	1024
Boston	0.857	0.714	0.355	49.748	5560	4713
Buffalo	0.961	0.971	0.528	54.342	2458	1849

Table 4.10
1980 White Male/White Female Earnings Difference by SMSA

SMSA	(1) Average Earnings Difference[a] (in logs)	(2) Earnings Difference Corrected for Selectivity Bias[b]	(3) Unexplained Earnings Difference[c] (in logs)	(4) Percent of Corrected Earnings Difference Unexplained[d]	Sample Size Men	Sample Size Women
Charleston	0.883	0.856	0.482	56.326	595	489
Charlotte	0.793	0.634	0.281	44.282	1200	1049
Chicago	0.953	0.914	0.573	62.656	12704	9840
Cincinnati	0.956	1.008	0.615	61.060	2565	1903
Cleveland	1.010	0.952	0.585	61.406	3671	2752
Columbia	0.737	0.837	0.617	73.795	611	572
Columbus	0.838	0.828	0.487	58.864	2150	1738
Dallas/Ft. Worth	0.930	0.833	0.505	60.347	5790	4730
Dayton	1.007	1.041	0.585	56.120	1552	1279
Detroit	1.101	1.106	0.642	58.061	8070	5726

79

Table 4.10
1980 White Male/White Female Earnings Difference by SMSA

SMSA	(1) Average Earnings Difference[a] (in logs)	(2) Earnings Difference Corrected for Selectivity Bias[b]	(3) Unexplained Earnings Difference[c] (in logs)	(4) Percent of Corrected Earnings Difference Unexplained[d]	Sample Size Men	Sample Size Women
Flint	1.130	1.075	0.569	52.955	997	706
Ft.Lauderdale	0.808	0.728	0.387	53.236	1776	1555
Gary	1.248	1.078	0.652	60.494	1262	791
Greensboro	0.714	0.817	0.538	65.887	1389	1219
Hartford	0.893	0.851	0.530	62.298	1530	1261
Houston	0.941	0.971	0.644	66.335	5622	4070
Indianapolis	0.981	1.042	0.645	61.851	2391	1896
Jackson	0.841	0.808	0.533	65.977	462	401
Jacksonville	0.876	0.830	0.490	59.012	1192	1021
KansasCity	0.918	0.885	0.542	61.211	2655	2220

Table 4.10
1980 White Male/White Female Earnings Difference by SMSA

SMSA	(1) Average Earnings Difference[a] (in logs)	(2) Earnings Difference Corrected for Selectivity Bias[b]	(3) Unexplained Earnings Difference[c] (in logs)	(4) Percent of Corrected Earnings Difference Unexplained[d]	Sample Size Men	Sample Size Women
Louisville	0.910	0.948	0.605	64.338	1854	1426
LA/Long Beach	0.726	0.827	0.574	69.462	11603	9106
Memphis	0.867	0.903	0.569	63.064	1064	898
Miami	0.713	0.773	0.497	64.286	2543	2269
Milwaukee	0.985	0.973	0.555	47.044	1988	2363
Mobile	0.967	1.064	0.650	61.068	712	516
Nashville	0.833	0.738	0.436	59.053	1615	1369
Nassau/Suffolk	1.067	1.111	0.689	62.011	5454	3913
NewOrleans	0.945	0.872	0.573	65.675	1834	1264
NewportNews	1.055	1.073	0.624	58.177	520	439

81

Table 4.10
1980 White Male/White Female Earnings Difference by SMSA

SMSA	(1) Average Earnings Difference[a] (in logs)	(2) Earnings Difference Corrected for Selectivity Bias[b]	(3) Unexplained Earnings Difference[c] (in logs)	(4) Percent of Corrected Earnings Difference Unexplained[d]	Sample Size Men	Sample Size Women
New York	0.665	0.660	0.395	59.820	13515	10885
Newark	0.926	1.056	0.710	67.201	3566	2712
Norfolk	1.007	0.862	0.385	44.702	787	728
Orlando	0.843	0.833	0.518	62.132	1314	1099
Philadelphia	0.930	0.947	0.501	62.396	8248	6342
Pittsburgh	1.017	0.977	0.597	61.142	4743	3250
Richmond	0.920	0.859	0.423	49.245	1120	892
Rochester	0.975	1.091	0.654	59.923	2012	1571
St.Louis	0.986	0.970	0.608	62.744	4471	3451
SanAntonio	0.823	0.748	0.360	48.152	1612	1373

82

Table 4.10
1980 White Male/White Female Earnings Difference by SMSA

SMSA	(1) Average Earnings Difference[a] (in logs)	(2) Earnings Difference Corrected for Selectivity Bias[b]	(3) Unexplained Earnings Difference[c] (in logs)	(4) Percent of Corrected Earnings Difference Unexplained[d]	Sample Size Men	Sample Size Women
SanDiego	0.883	0.860	0.505	58.718	2893	2335
SanFrancisco	0.798	0.831	0.528	63.613	5480	4506
Shreveport	0.870	0.819	0.510	62.236	535	430
Tampa/St.Pete	0.795	0.841	0.567	67.467	2483	2232
Toledo	1.110	1.178	0.756	64.221	1622	1188
WashingtonD.C.	0.808	0.770	0.394	51.230	4910	4224
Wilmington	1.013	1.016	0.594	58.430	806	594
UnitedStates	0.905	0.867	0.509	58.695	40357	32490

a $\overline{lnW}_a - \overline{lnW}_b$

b $\overline{lnW}_a - \overline{lnW}_b - [b'_a\overline{LAMBDA}_a - b'_b\overline{LAMBDA}_B]$

c $[\overline{X}_b(\beta'_a - \beta'_b)]$

d $\{[\overline{X}_b(\beta'_a - \beta'_b)]/[\overline{lnW}_a - \overline{lnW}_b - (b'_a \overline{LAMBDA}_a - b'_b \overline{LAMBDA}_b)]\}*100$

The first two tables, 4.7 and 4.8, show the wage decomposition estimates for black males. In 1970, 27 of the 56 wage differences rose after correcting for sample selection bias. In 1980, 14 such estimates rose. In comparing the unexplained portions of the wage differences, it can be seen that in 42 of the 56 cases, the unexplained portions fell between 1970 and 1980.[5] In 82% of the SMSA's, the unexplained portion of the earnings differential fell over the ten year period, an interesting finding in light of the deterioration of general economic conditions in the U.S. during the same time period.

Tables 4.9 and 4.10 give the results of the estimates for the white female / white male earnings differentials. In this case, 21 of the 56 estimates in 1970 rose after correcting for sample selection bias, while in 1980, 24 of the estimates rose. When comparing the percentage of the wage difference unexplained by productivity-related characteristics between 1970 and 1980, it can be seen that 31 of the 56 estimates fell.

Following other examples in the literature, this study concentrates on the residual (i.e., unexplained) component of the wage differential, since this is what is commonly referred to as an upper bound estimate of wage discrimination. To illustrate how the SMSA's compare with one another (and the U.S. as a whole), the percentage of the corrected wage difference unexplained by worker characteristics is ranked from highest to lowest in both 1970 and 1980. This is shown for blacks in table 4.11 and for women in table 4.12.

Having calculated these estimates for wage discrimination, the decennial change may then be computed for each SMSA. These changes are reported in table 4.13 for black males and in table 4.14 for women. The first column in each table gives the actual 1970–1980 change in the unexplained portion of the corrected wage difference, while the second column expresses this change as a percentage change.

Table 4.11 Percent of the Black/White Male Earnings Difference Unexplained by Worker Characteristics: SMSA's Ranked in Descending Order				
1970 Black/White Male Earnings Difference		1980 Black/White Male Earnings Difference	
SMSA	Percent Earnings Difference Explained	SMSA	Percent Earnings Difference Unexplained
Louisville	83.966	Buffalo	75.667
Indianapolis	82.074	Nassau/Suffolk	71.102
Hartford	80.511	Jackson	70.290
BatonRouge	79.443	Mobile	70.075
Beaumont	78.103	Columbia	69.489
Cincinnati	76.929	Nashville	67.124
Nashville	76.728	Charlotte	65.303
Nassau/Suffolk	73.839	Boston	64.905
Charleston	73.758	Greensboro	64.110
Wilmington	73.635	NewportNews	62.333
Ft.Lauderdale	72.811	Toledo	61.804
Gary	72.714	Flint	61.326
Orlando	72.636	Ft. Lauderdale	60.458
SanAntonio	70.589	Hartford	60.344
NewOrleans	70.154	Orlando	59.776
Shreveport	70.154	Columbus	58.149
Norfolk	69.939	SanAntonio	57.800

Table 4.11
Percent of the Black/White Male Earnings Difference Unexplained
by Worker Characteristics: SMSA's Ranked in Descending Order

1970 Black/White Male Earnings Difference		1980 Black/White Male Earnings Difference	
SMSA	Percent Earnings Difference Explained	SMSA	Percent Earnings Difference Unexplained
Miami	69.762	SanFrancisco	57.144
Akron	69.473	NewOrleans	57.109
Dayton	67.858	Louisville	53.592
LA/LongBeach	67.446	Dayton	51.772
Tampa/St.Pete	66.890	Tampa/St.Pete	51.597
Columbus	64.428	Newark	48.888
St.Louis	64.002	Cincinnati	47.188
KansasCity	63.974	La/LongBeach	46.458
Birmingham	61.871	NewYork	45.482
Toledo	61.396	Richmond	45.099
Memphis	60.427	Charleston	45.092
Cleveland	60.260	Pittsburgh	43.665
Houston	59.876	Milwaukee	43.287
Charlotte	59.146	Dallas/Ft.Worth	42.297
Chicago	58.813	SanDiego	42.228
Columbia	58.236	Wilmington	42.170
Dallas/Ft.Worth	57.878	Memphis	40.025

Table 4.11
Percent of the Black/White Male Earnings Difference Unexplained by Worker Characteristics: SMSA's Ranked in Descending Order

1970 Black/White Male Earnings Difference		1980 Black/White Male Earnings Difference	
SMSA	Percent Earnings Difference Explained	SMSA	Percent Earnings Difference Unexplained
Rochester	57.701	KansasCity	38.430
Baltimore	56.416	Baltimore	38.267
*United States	56.050	Houston	35.500
Boston	55.903	St.Louis	34.632
Flint	55.569	Norfolk	33.787
Greensboro	55.310	*United States	31.575
Richmond	52.928	Jacksonville	29.663
Mobile	51.581	Gary	29.588
Washington,D.C.	50.270	Rochester	29.039
Jackson	50.205	Birmingham	28.010
Detroit	50.133	Indianapolis	24.291
Milwaukee	49.071	WashingtonD.C.	18.357
Philadelphia	48.014	Detroit	14.305
Jacksonville	47.476	Philadelphia	14.209
SanFrancisco	47.039	Miami	5.560
NewYork	46.506	Chicago	2.028
Buffalo	46.481	Atlanta	-2.934

Table 4.11
Percent of the Black/White Male Earnings Difference Unexplained by Worker Characteristics: SMSA's Ranked in Descending Order

1970 Black/White Male Earnings Difference		1980 Black/White Male Earnings Difference	
SMSA	Percent Earnings Difference Explained	SMSA	Percent Earnings Difference Unexplained
Atlanta	42.124	BatonRouge	-6.237
NewportNews	39.889	Cleveland	-8.084
Newark	38.405	Shreveport	-66.073
Pittsburgh	32.245	Akron	-81.284
SanDiego	23.600	Beaumont	-210.400

Table 4.12
Percent of the White Male/Female Earnings Difference Unexplained by Worker Characteristics: SMSA's Ranked in Descending Order

1970 White Male/Female Earnings Difference		1980 White Male/Female Earnings Difference	
SMSA	Percent Earnings Difference Unexplained	SMSA	Percent Earnings Difference Unexplained
Gary	70.167	Columbia	73.795
Miami	69.475	LA/LongBeach	69.462
BatonRouge	68.555	Tampa/St.Pete	67.467
Louisville	68.258	Akron	67.404
Buffalo	68.199	Newark	67.201

Table 4.12
Percent of the White Male/Female Earnings Difference Unexplained
by Worker Characteristics: SMSA's Ranked in Descending Order

1970 White Male/Female Earnings Difference		1980 White Male/Female Earnings Difference	
SMSA	Percent Earnings Difference Unexplained	SMSA	Percent Earnings Difference Unexplained
Ft.Lauderdale	68.097	Houston	66.335
Birmingham	67.493	Jackson	65.977
Baltimore	67.049	Greensboro	65.887
Toledo	66.772	NewOrleans	65.675
Wilmington	66.445	Louisville	64.338
Milwaukee	65.635	Miami	64.286
Indianapolis	65.347	Toledo	64.221
NewYork	64.812	SanFrancisco	63.613
Beaumont	64.604	Memphis	63.064
Orlando	64.582	St.Louis	62.744
Hartford	63.972	Chicago	62.656
St.Louis	63.735	Philadelphia	62.396
Philadelphia	63.645	Hartford	62.298
Cincinnati	63.515	Shreveport	62.236
Akron	63.288	Orlando	62.132
NewOrleans	63.115	Nassau/Suffolk	62.011
Newark	62.444	Indianapolis	61.851

Table 4.12
Percent of the White Male/Female Earnings Difference Unexplained
by Worker Characteristics: SMSA's Ranked in Descending Order

1970 White Male/Female Earnings Difference		1980 White Male/Female Earnings Difference	
SMSA	Percent Earnings Difference Unexplained	SMSA	Percent Earnings Difference Unexplained
Detroit	62.154	Cleveland	61.406
*UnitedStates	61.428	KansasCity	61.211
Rochester	61.398	Pittsburgh	61.142
Cleveland	61.031	Mobile	61.068
Flint	60.890	Cincinnati	61.060
LA/LongBeach	60.778	Gary	60.494
Pittsburgh	60.478	Dallas/Ft.Worth	60.347
Nashville	59.693	Beaumont	60.230
Nassau	59.437	Rochester	59.923
Boston	59.255	NewYork	59.820
Charleston	59.245	Atlanta	59.398
Shreveport	59.222	Nashville	59.053
Tampa/St.Pete	59.149	Jacksonville	59.012
Columbus	59.132	BatonRouge	58.916
Chicago	59.109	Columbus	58.864
SanFrancisco	58.298	SanDiego	58.718
Dayton	58.133	*UnitedStates	58.695

Table 4.12
Percent of the White Male/Female Earnings Difference Unexplained by Worker Characteristics: SMSA's Ranked in Descending Order

1970 White Male/Female Earnings Difference		1980 White Male/Female Earnings Difference	
SMSA	Percent Earnings Difference Unexplained	SMSA	Percent Earnings Difference Unexplained
Houston	57.653	Wilmington	58.430
Charlotte	57.373	NewportNews	58.177
Richmond	56.850	Detroit	58.061
Jacksonville	56.336	Baltimore	57.512
Columbia	56.317	Charleston	56.326
SanDiego	55.588	Dayton	56.120
Dallas/Ft.Worth	55.038	Buffalo	54.342
KansasCity	53.888	Ft.Lauderdale	53.236
Atlanta	52.743	Flint	52.955
Memphis	50.685	Birmingham	52.628
Greensboro	49.902	WashingtonD.C.	51.230
SanAntonio	47.654	Boston	49.748
Norfolk	47.298	Richmond	49.245
WashingtonD.C.	46.386	SanAntonio	48.152
Jackson	46.315	Milwaukee	47.044
Mobile	41.436	Norfolk	44.702
NewportNews	36.087	Charlotte	44.282

AGGREGATE WAGE MODEL

This section employs the earnings model and decomposition of the previous sections to aid in analyzing the possible impact that local labor market characteristics have on the relative economic status of black men and white women (referred to collectively in this section as "minority workers"). In particular, we focus on the relationship between certain labor market characteristics and the percentage of the wage differential unexplained by worker traits.

Table 4.13 1970-1980 Change in the Unexplained Portion of the Black/White Male Earnings Difference by SMSA		
SMSA	Actual Change	Percentage Change
Akron	-150.757	-217.001
Atlanta	-39.190	-106.965
Baltimore	-18.149	-32.170
BatonRouge	-85.680	-107.851
Beaumont	-288.503	-369.389
Birmingham	-33.861	-54.729
Boston	9.002	16.103
Buffalo	29.186	62.791
Charleston	-28.666	-38.864
Charlotte	6.157	10.409
Chicago	-56.785	-96.551
Cincinnati	-29.741	-38.661

Table 4.13
1970-1980 Change in the Unexplained Portion of the Black/White Male Earnings Difference by SMSA

SMSA	Actual Change	Percentage Change
Cleveland	-69.100	-113.415
Columbia	11.253	19.323
Columbus	-6.279	-9.745
Dallas/Ft.Worth	-15.581	-26.921
Dayton	-16.086	-23.706
Detroit	-35.828	-71.466
Flint	5.757	10.361
Ft.Lauderdale	-12.353	-16.965
Gary	-43.226	-59.365
Greensboro	8.800	15.910
Hartford	-20.164	-25.049
Houston	-24.376	-40.711
Indianapolis	-57.783	-70.403
Jackson	20.085	40.007
Jacksonville	-17.816	-37.521
KansasCity	-25.544	-39.929
Louisville	-30.374	-36.174
LA/LongBeach	-20.988	-31.118
Memphis	-20.402	-33.762

Table 4.13 1970-1980 Change in the Unexplained Portion of the Black/White Male Earnings Difference by SMSA		
SMSA	Actual Change	Percentage Change
Miami	-64.202	-92.031
Milwaukee	-5.784	-11.788
Mobile	18.494	35.855
Nashville	-9.604	-12.517
Nassau/Suffolk	-2.737	-3.706
NewOrleans	-13.045	-18.595
NewportNews	22.444	56.265
NewYork	-1.024	-2.204
Newark	10.483	27.297
Norfolk	-36.152	-51.690
Orlando	-12.860	-17.705
Philadelphia	-33.805	-70.406
Pittsburgh	11.420	35.419
Richmond	-7.829	-14.792
Rochester	-28.662	-49.672
St.Louis	-29.370	-45.890
SanAntonio	-12.789	-18.118
SanDiego	18.768	80.002
SanFrancisco	10.105	21.481
Shreveport	-136.227	-194.183

Table 4.13
1970-1980 Change in the Unexplained Portion of the Black/White Male Earnings Difference by SMSA

SMSA	Actual Change	Percentage Change
Tampa/St.Pete	-15.293	-22.864
Toledo	0.408	0.664
WashingtonD.C.	-31.913	-63.484
Wilmington	-31.465	-42.731
UnitedStates.	-24.475	-43.666

Table 4.14
1970-1980 Change in the Unexplained Portion of the White Male/Female Earnings Difference by SMSA

SMSA	Actual Change	Percentage Change
Akron	4.116	6.503
Atlanta	6.655	12.619
Baltimore	-9.537	-14.225
BatonRouge	-9.639	-14.060
Beaumont	-4.374	-6.770
Birmingham	-14.865	-22.024
Boston	-9.507	-16.044
Buffalo	-13.850	-20.318
Charleston	-2.919	-4.929
Charlotte	-13.091	-22.817

Table 4.14
1970-1980 Change in the Unexplained Portion of the White Male/Female Earnings Difference by SMSA

SMSA	Actual Change	Percentage Change
Chicago	3.547	6.001
Cincinnati	-2.450	-3.866
Cleveland	0.375	0.615
Columbia	17.478	31.036
Columbus	-0.268	-0.454
Dallas/Ft.Worth	5.309	9.646
Dayton	-2.013	-3.463
Detroit	-4.093	-6.585
Flint	-7.935	-13.032
Ft.Lauderdale	-14.861	-21.824
Gary	-9.673	-13.786
Greensboro	15.985	32.034
Hartford	-1.674	-2.617
Houston	8.682	15.059
Indianapolis	-3.496	-5.351
Jackson	19.662	42.453
Jacksonville	2.676	4.751
KansasCity	7.323	13.589
Louisville	-3.920	-5.743
LA/LongBeach	8.684	14.288

Table 4.14		
1970-1980 Change in the Unexplained Portion of the White Male/Female Earnings Difference by SMSA		
SMSA	Actual Change	Percentage Change
Memphis	12.379	24.423
Miami	-5.189	-7.468
Milwaukee	-18.591	-28.325
Mobile	19.632	47.378
Nashville	-0.640	-1.072
Nassau/Suffolk	2.574	4.331
NewOrleans	2.560	4.057
NewportNews	22.090	61.215
NewYork	-4.992	-7.702
Newark	4.757	7.618
Norfolk	-2.596	-5.490
Orlando	-2.450	-3.795
Philadelphia	-1.249	-1.962
Pittsburgh	0.664	1.099
Richmond	-7.605	-13.377
Rochester	-1.475	-2.402
St.Louis	-0.991	-1.554
SanAntonio	0.490	1.047
SanDiego	3.130	5.631
SanFrancisco	5.315	9.118

Table 4.14 1970-1980 Change in the Unexplained Portion of the White Male/Female Earnings Difference by SMSA		
SMSA	Actual Change	Percentage Change
Shreveport	3.014	5.089
Tampa/St.Pete	8.318	14.063
Toledo	-2.551	-3.821
WashingtonD.C.	4.844	10.442
Wilmington	-8.015	-12.062
UnitedStates	-2.733	-4.449

Local Labor Market Conditions. A vector of characteristics is specified as being a proxy for measuring conditions in a particular labor market. These specified variables are hypothesized to influence our estimates of wage discrimination.

The white male unemployment rate is used as a measure of the employment opportunities for the favored group in the SMSA. Assuming a taste for discrimination against minority workers, it is possible that as the white male unemployment rate falls, the number of available preferred workers will also fall (this possibility was discussed in Chapter III). Employers may then find it more difficult to hire preferred types of workers. Competition for jobs has changed such that employers may be more inclined to hire and promote minority workers. This implies that minority workers may be afforded better wage opportunities with reductions in the white male unemployment rate, ceteris paribus. Hence it is hypothesized that an increase (decrease) in the white male unemployment rate will be associated with a rise (reduction) in our estimates of wage discrimination.

The percentage of the SMSA workforce that is unionized may have a positive or negative impact on the relative wages of minority workers. A number of studies have found that, in terms of wage gains, black males tend to benefit more from union membership than their white counterparts (see Hirsch and Addison 1986; Ashenfelter 1972). If black males gain more from union membership, an increase in the unionization rate may then improve their relative economic status. On the other hand, if unions themselves discriminate (see Ashenfelter 1972) an increase in the unionization rate may, in fact, increase the level of discrimination against minorities in the SMSA. Thus, the effect that a change in the level of unionization has on the estimates of wage discrimination is not hypothesized a priori.

An increase in the proportion of the SMSA working age (minority) population that possesses at least a high school degree is expected to be associated with lower levels of discrimination. As the educational level of minorities becomes more similar to that of whites, it is expected that their rate of return to education should become more similar to that of whites. As this occurs, the portion of the wage differential attributable to differences in coefficients will become smaller, and hence, the estimate of discrimination should become smaller. Also, to the extent that employers engage in statistical discrimination, a more educated minority labor force (on average) may improve the employers expectation about hiring minority workers. This suggests that increases in the proportion of an SMSA's minority population with at least a high school diploma are expected to be associated with better wage and occupational opportunities, and hence, reductions in our estimates of discrimination.

The SMSA's minority labor force participation rate is proffered as a proxy for measuring the relative supply of these workers. Assuming some employers have a taste for discrimination against minority workers and that the number of minority workers exceeds the number of available jobs with nondiscriminating employers, equilibrium occurs where the wage of the minority group is less than that of the preferred group. This is because some of the minority workers are employed by discriminating employers (i.e., those with a positive discrimination coefficient) who require a wage differential in favor of the preferred group. If the relative supply of minority workers increases, there will be an excess supply of minority workers at the old wage differential. For equilibrium to be restored, the wage differential will rise as minority workers find jobs with the more discriminating firms (those with larger values of the discrimination coefficient), thereby increasing the effects of discrimination. As Becker (1971) explains, "If members of the same factor have different tastes for discrimination, an increase in the relative supply of non-whites [or women] increases the equilibrium market discrimination against them, even if all tastes remain fixed" (p. 117). It is, therefore, postulated that, an increase in the labor force participation rate of the minority worker group (i.e., an increase in their relative supply) will be associated with larger estimates of wage discrimination, ceteris paribus.

Relative shifts in labor demand will influence labor market opportunities available to all workers (including minorities). Conventional neoclassical theory suggests that changes in the demand for labor are directly associated with changes in wages. In general, labor demand is influenced by cyclical forces in the economy, and these forces need not affect all labor markets similarly. The cyclical shift in local labor demand can be approximated by the percentage change in total employment in different industries in a particular SMSA. For example, changes in the employment of the manufacturing and construction sectors are expected to have a large multiplier effect on labor markets through employment in the intermediate goods sector (see Beham 1978). A percentage increase in the employment of these sectors in the SMSA is likely to reflect expansionary forces and serve as a proxy for an increase in labor demand. In turn, it is hypothesized that this would increase wage opportunities, thereby, reducing our estimates of wage discrimination in the labor market.

In a similar vein, the change in the SMSA's population might also indicate whether labor market opportunities are growing or deteriorating over a given period. Typically those SMSA's that experienced moderate to rapid population growth from 1970 to 1980, have been characterized as expanding labor markets. As previously noted, expanding labor markets are expected to be associated with higher wage opportunities for minority workers. This would lead us to hypothesize that decennial population growth of an SMSA is associated with reductions in our estimates of wage discrimination, ceteris paribus.

Changes in transfer programs aimed at reducing poverty may also influence the relative economic status of minorities and hence, our estimates of wage discrimination. Changes in the number of individuals in an SMSA receiving Aid to Families with Dependent Children (AFDC) and the changes in these average monthly payments received by families in an SMSA are used to represent changes in antipoverty programs.

The effect of these changes on our estimates of discrimination is not clear, however. Assuming discrimination does exist, one possibility is that minority workers who are more able might drop out of the labor force and prefer non-wage alternatives. If more able individuals drop out of the labor force, then those who may be best able to overcome any disadvantages from labor market discrimination have left (Chiswick

1978).[6] If these workers abandon labor market activity, this may lead to larger empirical estimates of earnings discrimination. Another possibility is that those minority workers who would otherwise be expected to receive low wages (i.e., those with lower skills) would be the ones who would reduce their labor force attachment in favor of non-wage activities (see Butler and Heckman 1977; Brown 1984). This implies that the more able minority workers remain in the labor force, which might lower empirical estimates of wage discrimination. With these conflicting possibilities, we choose, a priori, not to assign a hypothetical sign to the welfare coefficients. Table 4.15 summarizes the variables and the hypothesized signs of the parameter coefficients of the aggregate model.

Table 4.15 Hypothesized Effects of Changes in Local Labor Market Variables on Estimates of Wage Discrimination	
(an increase in the) Local Labor Market Variable	Hypothesized Sign
White male unemployment rate	+
Labor force participation rate of black males	+
Labor force participation rate of white females	+
Percentage of the labor force unionized	?
Proportion of the black working age population having at least a high school diploma	-
Proportion of the female working age population having at least a high school diploma	-
Construction employment	-
Manufacturing employment	-
Population	-
Number of individuals receiving AFDC	?
Average AFDC payment per family	?

Empirical Results: Aggregate Model. The previous section outlined the explanatory variables to be used in assessing the relationship between changes in local labor market conditions and changes in the estimates of wage discrimination against black males and white females. In defining the change in each of the local market characteristics, the percentage change (denoted as %CHG) in each variable is used. This is done so that the magnitude of the change can be accounted for. For example, suppose in one SMSA the white male unemployment rate rises from a level of 4% in 1970 to 5% in 1980, while in another SMSA the same variable rises from 10% to 11% during the same time period. In absolute terms the two changes are equal, but in percentage terms the first SMSA experiences a 25% increase in its white male unemployment rate, while the second SMSA experiences a 10% rise. Using the percentage change does not, however, circumvent the problem discussed in Chapter III. That is, in our analysis the first labor market is assumed to experience a loosening, when, in fact, many economists would regard an unemployment rate of 5% as indicating a tight labor market. Since the variables are expressed in percentage terms, it is possible to interpret this aggregate model as a logarithmic specification.

Based on equation (3-9), the general form of the aggregate wage model can now be expressed as:

$$\Delta D_j = \pi_o + \pi_1 \Delta\alpha_{1j} + \pi_2 \Delta\alpha_{2j} + \ldots + \pi_k \Delta\alpha_{kj} + \epsilon$$

where the subscript j represents the jth SMSA, $\Delta\alpha_{1j}$, $\Delta\alpha_{2j}$, . . ., $\Delta\alpha_{kj}$ represents the percentage change in the k local labor market variables, and π_o, π_1, π_2, . . ., π_k are the parameters to be estimated. The dependent variable, ΔD_j, is the percentage change in the unexplained portion of the male/female (black/white) earnings differential. Ordinary least square estimation of the coefficients in above equation (i.e., equation 3–9) provide estimates of the direction of the relationship between the percentage change in the local labor market variable ($\Delta\alpha_k$) and the percentage change in estimates of wage discrimination against the minority group.

The results of this estimation for black males is given in table 4.16. At conventional levels of significance, the only significant coefficients are the percentage change in construction employment and the percentage change in the number of individuals receiving AFDC (one of our proxies for antipoverty programs). From the sign on the coefficient

	Table 4.16		
	Estimated Aggregate Equation Black/White Males		
Dependent Variable:	Percentage Change in the Unexplained Portion of Black/White Male Earnings Difference (Standard Errors in Parentheses)		
Exogenous Variable	Estimated Coefficient	Estimated Coefficient	Estimated Coefficient
Constant	-67.559*** (46.973)	-60.442 (44.932)	-66.162 (49.666)
%CHG WHITE MALE UNEMPLOYMENT RATE	-0.216 (0.211)	_0.061 (0.214)	-0.266 (0.196)
%CHG BLACK MALE LABOR FORCE PARTICIPATION RATE	-1.716 (2.933)		
%CHG SMSA UNION RATE	0.238 (0.457)	-0.033 (0.464)	0.229 (0.450)
%CHG IN PROPORTION OF BLACK MALES W/ HIGH SCHOOL DIPLOMA	0.006 (0.596)	0.073 (0.560)	0.175 (0.522)
%CHG IN SMSA POPULATION	0.759 (0.875)	0.569 (0.881)	
%CHG IN CONSTRUCTION EMPLOYMENT	-1.157*** (0.772)	-1.350** (0.744)	-1.064 (0.808)

Table 4.16 Estimated Aggregate Equation Black/White Males			
Dependent Variable:	Percentage Change in the Unexplained Portion of Black/White Male Earnings Difference (Standard Errors in Parentheses)		
Exogenous Variable	Estimated Coefficient	Estimated Coefficient	Estimated Coefficient
%CHG IN MANUFACTURING EMPLOYMENT	-0.725 (1.361)	-0.528 (1.319)	-0.571 (1.239)
%CHG IN # INDIVIDUALS RECEIVING AFDC	1.058* (0.384)		0.943* (0.380)
%CHG IN AVERAGE FAMILY AFDC PAYMENTS	0.194 (0.372)		0.349 (0.359)
%CHG IN BLACK SMSA POPULATION			0.396 (1.138)
R^2	0.2177	0.0699	0.1980

*Significant at the 5% level.
**Significant at the 10% level.
***Significant at the 15% level.

for AFDC recipients and payments, it seems that more liberal antipoverty programs are associated with increases in our estimates of wage discrimination. This suggests that as AFDC becomes more generous, lower wage blacks may drop out of the labor force, thus causing the selectivity corrected wage gap to widen.

The signs on the percentage change in construction and manufacturing employment coefficients are in the hypothesized direction, although manufacturing employment is not significant. The sign on the union coefficient indicates that there seems to be a positive (albeit insignificant) association between the rate of unionization and our estimates of wage discrimination.[7] The signs on the other coefficients appear to be contrary to that hypothesized in table 4.15. The results of this model suggest that changes in the proffered local labor market variables do not play a significant role in explaining changes in our estimates of wage discrimination against black males.

Alternative models for the aggregate equation are given in columns two and three in table 4.16. The model specified in the second column omits the variables concerning changes in black male labor force participation and AFDC. These variables were omitted because of the potential bias that may result from the labor force participation response of minority workers resulting from changes in antipoverty programs (see Butler and Heckman 1977; Brown 1984). This model, however, did not perform well in explaining the variation in changes of our estimates of wage discrimination.

In the model specified in the third column of table 4.16, the AFDC variables are reintroduced as explanatory variables. In addition, the percentage change in the black population of an SMSA is offered as a proxy for the relative supply of blacks. In this model, the only significant variable is the percentage change in the number of individuals receiving AFDC.

Turning to women, the results reported in table 4.17 are similar to those of black males. At conventional levels of significance, the percentage change in the white male unemployment rate is the only significant coefficient. The negative sign, however, is opposite that which was hypothesized. Interpretations of the coefficients in this model must be made with extreme caution since the model does not explain very well the variations in the dependent variable ($R^2 = .13$). Alternative models are specified in the second and third columns of the table. The results of these models, however, are similar to those reported in column one.

The results of these two wage models seem to indicate that our estimates of wage discrimination do not vary systematically with changes in local labor market conditions. It appears that estimates of wage discrimination against minorities are unaffected by measurable changes in local labor market conditions.

Assuming discrimination were to exist in a labor market, economists such as Shulman (1987, 1984a, 1984b) and Tobin (1965) have raised the possibility that minorities may fare better (in terms of discrimination) as economic conditions improve in a labor market. From the results of our analysis, we find no support for this proposition.

Instead, our results are more supportive of the neoclassical view. This view suggests that systematic differences in labor markets (which favor the economic status of one group over another) would equalize over time as workers become aware of these differences and react accordingly (e.g., through migration).

A second possibility also exists. Topel (1986) has shown that changes in local labor demand affect wages of workers in those areas, especially those who have the strongest attachment to the area, and who are least mobile (pp. S141–S142). From our results, it is possible that

Table 4.17 Estimated Aggregate Equation White Male/Female			
Dependent Variable:	Percentage Change in the Unexplained Portion of White Male/Female Earnings Difference (Standard Errors in Parentheses)		
Exogenous Variable	Estimated Coefficient	Estimated Coefficient	Estimated Coefficient
Constant	-10.912 (19.875)	-0.861 (11.659	-15.201 (14.805)
%CHG WHITE MALE UNEMPLOYMENT RATE	-0.082*** (0.056)	-0.068 (0.052)	-0.074** (0.050)
%CHG WHITE FEMALE LABOR FORCE PARTICIPATION RATE	0.481 (0.679		0.643 (0.602)
%CHG SMSA UNION RATE	0.142 (0.119)	0.102 (0.112)	0.108 (0.112)

Table 4.17 Estimated Aggregate Equation White Male/Female			
Dependent Variable:	Percentage Change in the Unexplained Portion of White Male/Female Earnings Difference (Standard Errors in Parentheses)		
Exogenous Variable	Estimated Coefficient	Estimated Coefficient	Estimated Coefficient
%CHG IN PROPORTION OF WHITE FEMALES W/ HIGH SCHOOL DIPLOMA	0.214 (0.476)	0.182 (0.451)	0.385 (0.379)
%CHG IN SMSA POPULATION	0.070 (0.210)	0.075 (0.187)	-0.011 (0.177)
%CHG IN CONSTRUCTION EMPLOYMENT	0.071 (0.231)	0.141 (0.197)	
%CHG IN MANUFACTURING EMPLOYMENT	-0.316 (0.346)	-0.288 (0.331)	
%CHG IN # INDIVIDUALS RECEIVING AFDC	0.077 (0.097)		
%CHG IN AVERAGE FAMILY AFDC PAYMENTS	-0.014 (0.098)		
R^2	0.1351	0.1097	0.1085

*Significant at the 5% level.
**Significant at the 10% level.
***Significant at the 15% level.

even with wage discrimination in a particular market, the wages of workers possessing similar skills would be affected in the same manner. Thus, if the wages of equally productive white males and minorities were affected in approximately the same manner, our estimates of discrimination might be invariant to such changes in local labor market conditions —implying no systematic relationship between changes in estimates of wage discrimination and changes in local labor market attributes.

SUMMARY

The basic objective of this Chapter was to develop a wage model that would allow us to empirically assess whether or not there is a systematic relationship between a conventional estimate of wage discrimination and changing attributes of local labor markets.

The hypothesis test presented above indicates that wage structures of workers vary significantly across SMSA's. The results of these tests confirm the appropriateness of the local labor market, as espoused by Hirsch (1979) and Hanushek (1981), versus an aggregate U.S. labor market employed in many other empirical studies. Within the context of a local labor market, we then explored sources of the black/white and male/female earnings differential for both 1970 and 1980. The unexplained portion of these earnings differentials (which analysts frequently attribute to earnings discrimination) were calculated for each SMSA.

We then discussed the possible link between changes in certain measurable local labor market conditions and changes in our estimates of earnings discrimination. An aggregate wage model was presented which attempted to test the direction of the hypothetical links between changes in local labor market characteristics and our estimates of wage discrimination. Specifically, we attempted to test whether women and blacks fare better or worse as labor markets improve or deteriorate, as has been suggested by Shulman (1987) and others. The results of our aggregate models suggest that there is no significant, systematic association between our estimates of wage discrimination and changes in local labor market conditions. The next Chapter explores whether changes in measurable local labor market conditions affect the relative occupational status of white women and black men.

V

The Occupational Distributions of Women and Blacks Relative to White Men

INTRODUCTION

In addition to examining relative wages, a complete investigation of the relative economic status of women and blacks should also explore how these groups fare with respect to occupational attainment. In Chapter IV, the analysis centered on estimating sources of the wage differential between the two groups relative to white men and how changes in labor market attributes might explain changes in these estimates. This Chapter concentrates on the possible relationship between the changes in the relative occupational status of these groups and changing labor market characteristics.

OCCUPATIONAL DISTRIBUTIONS WITHIN A NATIONAL VS. LOCAL LABOR MARKET

In examining the relative economic position of women and blacks, it is important to determine how the occupational distribution of workers varies across labor markets. Within this context, we again employ the SMSA as the local labor market. The observed occupational distributions are based on the following eleven occupational categories as used by the Census Bureau: Laborers, Transportation, Operatives, Craft, Private Household Service, Other Service, Clerical, Sales, Technical, Professional, and managerial. Table 5.1 gives a description of each of these occupational categories.

Table 5.1 Occupational Classifications	
Occupational Category	**Occupations Included**
1. Laborers	Handlers, Equipment Cleaners, Helpers, and Laborers
2. Transportation	Transportation and Material Moving Occupations
3. Operatives	Machine Operators, Assemblers, and Inspectors
4. Craft	Precision Production, Craft, and Repair Occupations
5. Private Household Service	Private Household Service Occupations
6. Other Service	Other Service Occupations
7. Clerical	Administrative Support Occupations, including Clerical
8. Sales	Sales Occupations
9. Technical	Technicians and Related Support Occupations
10. Professional	Professional Specialty Occupations
11. Managerial`	Executive, Administrative, and Managerial Occupations

Between 1970 and 1980, the Census Bureau changed its narrowly defined three-digit occupational classification system (Census 1983b, p. K30). The primary difference is that in 1980, the occupational coding system was adapted to the Standard Occupational Classification System, which was initially introduced in 1977. This change allowed many of the broad occupational categories of 1980 to be compatible with many of those in 1970, but "the principles governing the classification and many of the detailed categories have been altered substantially" (Census 1983b, p. K30). The eleven occupations specified in table 5.1 were the broadest possible for comparisons between 1970 and 1980. Also, since many of the SMSA's have sample sizes of approximately 100 (especially for black males), the eleven broad categories minimize the potential number of empty cells.

One method of examining whether SMSA occupational distributions vary from a national distribution is to make use of the chi-square goodness of fit test. The null hypothesis is that the occupational distribution of a particular group of workers in an SMSA is statistically equivalent to the corresponding national distribution. The national distribution is calculated from the 1/1000 national Public Use Samples in both 1970 and 1980. These national distributions are reported in tables 5.2 and 5.3. The null hypothesis may be tested by the following statistic (Siegel and Castellan 1988, p. 45):

$$(5\text{--}1) \quad \text{CHISQ} = \sum_{m=1}^{M} \frac{(P_m^{SMSA} - P_m^{natl})^2}{P_m^{natl}}$$

where $P_m^{SMSA} =$ the observed frequency of workers in the mth occupation from a given SMSA,

$P_m^{natl} =$ the observed frequency of workers in the mth occupation from the national (i.e., U.S.) distribution, and

M = the number of occupations (eleven).

The term, P_m^{natl}, represents the expected percentage of workers in the mth occupation when the null hypothesis is true. Under the null hypothesis, the distribution of CHISQ, as calculated from equation (5–1), follows a chi-square distribution with $(M–1)$ degrees of freedom. Rejection of the null hypothesis would indicate that the occupational distribution of a group of workers within the SMSA differs significantly from that of the United States, and would lend support to the notion that the U.S. may not generally be viewed as an aggregate labor market.

The results of the chi-square goodness of fit test for 1970 are reported in table 5.4. The null hypothesis is rejected in 5 of the 55 SMSA's for white men, in 21 SMSA's for black men, and in 4 SMSA's for white women. Table 5.5 reports the results for 1980. Here the null hypothesis is rejected in 4 SMSA's for white men, in 14 SMSA's for black men, and in 3 SMSA's for white women. These results indicate (especially in the case of black men) that in some instances the occupational distributions of an SMSA differ significantly from that of the nation as a whole. The results of the chi-square tests lend support to the use of local labor markets in comparing the relative occupational distributions of workers.

Table 5.2 National Occupational Distributions in 1970[a]			
Occupation	Percent White Males	Percent Black Males	Percent White Females
Laborers	5.5	17.1	1.0
Private Household	0.0	0.5	1.7
Other Service	6.4	14.8	15.3
Operatives	15.0	22.6	15.7
Transportation	6.5	11.4	0.5
Clerical	8.1	7.9	37.7
Craft	24.8	16.1	1.7
Sales	7.0	2.0	7.8
Technical	4.1	1.3	2.0
Professional	10.8	3.7	13.3
Managerial	11.7	2.6	3.3
[a]based on the 1/1000 Public Use Sample			

Table 5.3 National Occupational Distributions in 1980[a]			
Occupation	Percent White Males	Percent Black Males	Percent White Females
Laborers	5.9	13.6	2.3
Private Household Service	0.0	0.2	0.7
Other Service	7.1	15.6	14.7
Operatives	11.2	17.8	9.8
Transportation	8.3	12.6	1.0
Clerical	6.9	9.0	33.5
Craft	23.5	15.9	2.3
Sales	9.0	3.7	10.9
Technical	3.2	1.9	2.9
Professional	10.6	4.8	14.2
Managerial	14.2	4.9	7.6
[a]based on the 1/1000 Public Use Sample			

The above test gives a general indication of whether or not the U.S. may be viewed as a homogeneous aggregate labor market. Although the occupational distributions may vary across SMSA's, it may be that certain occupations have a national labor market while others a local market. Some authors have asserted that the market for occupations employing college-educated individuals may be a national market. For instance, Hanushek (1981) points to this conclusion when he notes that college-educated individuals are more mobile and display less variation in their returns to human capital variables. On the other hand, there is evidence which suggests that the market for occupations employing manual workers may be more of a localized one (Goodman 1970, p. 188).

A general indication of which occupations employ more mobile workers can be obtained from examination of migration data in each of the eleven occupations. For each occupation, we can tabulate the percentage of black male, white male, and white female workers who, in 1980, resided in the same SMSA as they did in 1975. These tabulations are reported in table 5.6. The first three columns are tabulated from the 1/1000 Public Use Sample. The fourth column is the percentage of each occupational group who resided in the same county in both 1975 and 1980. This figure, calculated for both sexes and all races, is provided as a comparison measure for our tabulations. In each case, it appears that the managerial, professional, technical and sales occupations are the most mobile occupations, although the majority of workers in all occupational categories resided in the same SMSA/county in both 1975 and 1980.

The results of the chi-square test, along with the occupational mobility tabulations, provide general support to the employment of the SMSA as our local occupational labor market. The chi-square analysis suggests that for some SMSA's, there appears to be significant differences between the local and national occupational distributions; the mobility tabulations indicate that the majority of workers retained the same SMSA residence between 1970 and 1980. Thus, the SMSA (treated as a separate labor market) will be the basis of our analysis in assessing the possible relationship between changes in labor market conditions and the relative occupational status of women and blacks.

INDEX OF DISSIMILARITY

Since there is no absolute standard for measuring or estimating the extent of occupational segregation, we appeal to the occupational attainment literature. A technique frequently used as a segregation measure involves calculating what is known as the "index of dissimilarity" (see Chapter III, equation 3-11). Recall that this index (also called the occupational segregation index) is defined as:

$$S = \frac{1}{2} \sum_{m=1}^{M} |P_{Am} - P_{Bm}|$$

Table 5.4 1970 Occupational Distributions CHI-SQUARE Goodness of Fit[a]			
SMSA	White Men	Black Men	White Women
Akron	10.44	50.66*	3.43
Atlanta	5.31	3.66	3.01
Baltimore	1.22	5.05	1.09
Baton Rouge	8.78	24.52*	18.11*
Beaumont	15.91*	23.92*	17.18*
Birmingham	4.45	9.13	4.43
Boston	1.53	9.28	1.75
Buffalo	5.50	27.83*	3.11
Charleston	7.51	32.14*	5.99
Charlotte	11.13	9.05	5.23
Chicago	0.45	1.57	1.44
Cincinnati	3.63	5.11	1.60
Cleveland	3.26	4.85	0.76
Columbia	8.90	4.61	3.58
Columbus	1.27	3.98	1.08
Dallas/Ft. Worth	1.76	6.50	1.40
Dayton	6.40	15.05	1.71
Detroit	3.31	30.22*	2.64
Flint	29.11*	52.10*	14.18
Ft. Lauderdale	13.99	38.86*	5.69
Gary	16.16*	18.89*	9.16

Table 5.4 1970 Occupational Distributions CHI-SQUARE Goodness of Fit[a]			
SMSA	White Men	Black Men	White Women
Greensboro	3.34	10.88	30.97*
Hartford	1.47	10.93	1.95
Houston	1.53	12.17	4.46
Indianapolis	3.05	4.74	1.51
Jackson	17.69*	39.50*	4.77
Jacksonville	5.38	14.71	6.58
Kansas City	2.16	7.48	1.12
Louisville	8.42	13.08	3.06
LA/Long Beach	0.75	6.00	1.03
Memphis	6.01	5.76	3.36
Miami	4.19	17.68*	13.62
Milwaukee	4.20	35.78*	3.42
Mobile.	1.55	26.06*	3.23
Nashville	2.07	14.47	1.04
Nassau/Suffolk	6.39	9.33	2.54
NewOrleans	1.66	7.91	6.18
Newport News	13.01	20.84*	9.37
New York	7.98	13.18	4.27
Newark	2.14	5.20	2.94
Norfolk	7.37	17.94*	5.47
Orlando	7.39	21.88*	6.40

Table 5.4			
1970 Occupational Distributions CHI-SQUARE Goodness of Fit[a]			
SMSA	White Men	Black Men	White Women
Philadelphia	0.81	0.67	1.32
Pittsburgh	5.47	5.33	5.68
Richmond	6.32	5.34	6.02
Rochester	2.60	15.52*	4.89
St. Louis	1.98	3.93	0.88
San Antonio	3.75	16.48*	4.33
San Diego	3.53	14.45	8.43
San Francisco	1.73	3.65	3.13
Shreveport	2.83	15.06	6.55
Tampa/St. Pete	4.08	24.11*	3.04
Toledo	7.52	18.23*	3.84
Washington D.C.	31.07*	20.83*	17.13*
Wilmington	5.28	6.02	2.38

H$_o$:   the occupational distribution in the Jth SMSA is statistically equivalent to the national distribution (based on the 1/1000 Public Use Sample)

*The null hypothesis is rejected at the .10 significance level (the critical value for 10 degrees of freedom is 15.98)

| Table 5.5 | | | |
| 1980 Occupational Distributions CHI-SQUARE Goodness of Fit[a] | | | |
SMSA	White Men	Black Men	White Women
Akron	9.13	15.02	6.10
Atlanta	3.57	1.55	1.05
Baltimore	1.51	2.36	0.39
Baton Rouge	7.96	5.41	4.20
Beaumont	22.01*	21.54*	13.23
Birmingham	5.87	13.14	2.52
Boston	3.85	21.64*	3.15
Buffalo	8.46	21.82*	3.00
Charleston	6.52	13.29	5.04
Charlotte	3.51	6.61	26.12*
Chicago	0.39	1.05	0.82
Cincinnati	3.42	5.20	2.24
Cleveland	2.95	6.90	0.96
Columbia	6.58	12.53	1.82
Columbus	0.99	6.55	0.53
Dallas/Ft. Worth	2.25	5.00	1.38
Dayton	6.43	10.76	2.24
Detroit	7.42	22.23*	2.89
Flint	41.11*	56.54*	21.82*

| Table 5.5 | | | |
| 1980 Occupational Distributions CHI-SQUARE Goodness of Fit[a] | | | |
SMSA	White Men	Black Men	White Women
Ft. Lauderdale	9.15	11.21	3.94
Gary	22.07*	17.58*	9.54
Greensboro	6.61	9.31	48.32*
Hartford	2.42	10.90	2.00
Houston	4.08	9.21	4.63
Indianapolis	4.10	11.01	1.59
Jackson	14.14	11.10	10.89
Jacksonville	3.61	19.67*	3.22
Kansas City	1.45	3.04	0.53
Louisville	9.02	10.00	4.04
LA/Long Beach	0.71	4.03	2.19
Memphis	3.03	12.75	3.21
Miami	4.36	7.23	4.55
Milwaukee	3.90	29.58*	3.53
Mobile	7.28	12.79	5.62
Nashville	0.75	8.03	3.47
Nassau/Suffolk	4.99	12.32	2.61
New Orleans	1.67	12.18	7.08
Newport News	7.74	7.37	9.34
New York	7.49	8.70	9.97
Newark	1.85	1.90	3.10

Table 5.5 1980 Occupational Distributions CHI-SQUARE Goodness of Fit[a]			
SMSA	White Men	Black Men	White Women
Norfolk	7.87	11.56	9.56
Orlando	4.16	14.86	2.81
Philadelphia	0.17	0.54	0.61
Pittsburgh	5.75	5.60	4.26
Richmond	3.63	5.10	4.80
Rochester	5.18	14.94	6.55
St. Louis	1.73	3.49	1.01
San Antonio	4.68	17.11*	3.62
San Diego	5.04	21.05*	4.18
San Francisco	2.89	8.95	3.23
Shreveport	6.69	17.68*	4.84
Tampa/St. Pete	3.82	14.88	2.00
Toledo	15.39	20.34*	7.98
Washington D.C.	27.19*	19.65*	14.99
Wilmington	2.94	25.47*	2.03

H_o: the occupational distribution in the Jth SMSA is statistically equivalent to the national distribution (based on the 1/1000 Public Use Sample)

*The null hypothesis is rejected at the .10 significance level (the critical value for 10 degrees of freedom is 15.98)

	Table 5.6 Occupational Mobility			
	Percent in each occupation who resided in same SMSA in 1975 and 1980[a]			Percent in each occupation who resided in same county in 1975 and 1980[b]
Occupation	White Men	Black Men	White Women	Both Sexes/All Races
Laborers	89	90	87	85
Transportation	88	92	89	84
Operatives	90	91	90	88
Craft	88	90	85	83
Private Household Service	78	100	81	90
Other Service	91	92	84	84
Clerical	86	88	85	82
Sales	82	91	82	78
Technical	80	83	84	73
Professional	81	83	81	73
Managerial	80	85	82	75

[a]based on the 1/1000 Public Use Sample
[b]1980 U.S. Census Subject Report, "Geographical Mobility for States and the Nation," 1948, p.35

where P_{am} is the percentage of the white male workforce in occupation m, and P_{bm} is the percentage of the black male, or white female workforce in occupation m. The value of the index is based on the absolute deviation in the percentage employed in each occupation and indicates the percentage of a given group that would have to shift between jobs to equalize the two occupational distributions. S can range from zero to 100; a zero value indicates equal proportions of the two groups of workers in each category (i.e., no segregation), while a value of 100 indicates total segregation by race or sex.

The value of the index may depend upon the level of aggregation of the occupations. Generally, the higher the level of aggregation (the fewer the number of occupations) the smaller the measure of segregation. Thus, when comparing S over time, the same number of jobs at the same level of aggregation should be used (see Beller 1985 and England 1981 for a discussion of this issue). In addition, the index does not allow judgments to be made on the basis of the quality of job distributions—e.g., that the distribution of one group is "better" or "worse" than that of another. The index only assesses the degree to which job distributions between two groups of workers are dissimilar (Albelda 1986, p. 405). Based on the eleven occupational categories outlined in Table 5.1, the black/white and male/female index is calculated for each of the SMSA's in both 1970 and 1980.

Tables 5.7 and 5.8 give the occupational segregation index for black and white males in 1970 and 1980, respectively, while Tables 5.9 and 5.10 report those for white men and women. The second and third column in each of the tables lists the sample size for the two groups in question. The last entry in each of the tables gives an index value, calculated for the U.S. as a whole. For black men relative to white men, the index ranged from a value of 51.65 to 24.60 in 1970, whereas the range in 1980 was 44.15 to 19.35. Over the ten year period, the index fell in 49 SMSA's and rose in 6.

Turning to women (Tables 5.9 and 5.10), the index ranged from 61.25 to 40.20 in 1970, and 55.9 to 33.05 in 1980. In all but one SMSA, the index of dissimilarity fell in the decade between 1970 and 1980. In Mobile, the index rose by a marginal amount (.05) during that time period.

When comparing the indexes of black males to that of white females, it can be seen that, on average, the index of women exceeds that of black men. This is consistent with findings by other researchers (see Albelda 1986; King 1992; Lyson 1985, as a few examples). This suggests that more workers (i.e., white women, white men or a combination of the two) would have to change jobs in order for the white female

Table 5.7 1970 Black Male/White Male Occupational Segregation Index by SMSA			
SMSA	Index of Dissimilarity (S)	Sample Size White Men	Sample Size Black Men
Akron	38.65	1395	99
Atlanta	43.05	2429	601
Baltimore	37.20	3457	893
Baton Rouge	44.90	410	127
Beaumont	45.10	526	123
Birmingham	38.35	1109	348
Boston	30.45	7204	224
Buffalo	36.35	2640	200
Charleston	38.45	351	128
Charlotte	47.70	692	191
Chicago	33.20	12848	2183
Cincinnati	32.15	2537	263
Cleveland	34.00	3931	613
Columbia	47.05	443	119
Columbus	33.60	1626	184
Dallas/Ft. Worth	43.90	4417	591
Dayton	26.15	1652	162
Detroit	36.20	7620	1499
Flint	30.05	951	123
Ft. Lauderdale	48.10	1007	128
Gary	24.60	1209	199

	Table 5.7		
	1970 Black Male/White Male Occupational Segregation Index by SMSA		
SMSA	Index of Dissimilarity (S)	Sample Size White Men	Sample Size Black Men
Greensboro	37.35	1098	204
Hartford	32.65	1729	111
Houston	39.30	3659	695
Indianapolis	30.10	2129	258
Jackson	51.65	308	127
Jacksonville	43.95	818	172
Kansas City	33.75	2404	260
Louisville	29.20	1565	168
LA/Long Beach	28.25	13144	1369
Memphis	43.30	1012	409
Miami	46.75	2146	335
Milwaukee	34.15	2816	185
Mobile	43.05	539	169
Nashville	38.45	973	159
Nassau/Suffolk	35.70	5074	187
New Orleans	42.10	1510	508
Newport News	39.75	423	113
New York	24.85	15381	3120
Newark	38.50	3325	649
Norfolk	47.05	834	283
Orlando	42.45	728	94

	Table 5.7		
1970 Black Male/White Male Occupational Segregation Index by SMSA			
SMSA	Index of Dissimilarity (S)	Sample Size White Men	Sample Size Black Men
Philadelphia	30.45	6565	1410
Pittsburgh	28.40	4892	278
Richmond	47.95	886	239
Rochester	38.10	1733	111
St. Louis	38.95	4250	584
San Antonio	27.80	1313	92
San Diego	33.95	2076	82
San Francisco	31.95	5725	606
Shreveport	47.75	380	142
Tampa/St. Pete	43.65	1502	182
Toledo	33.95	1346	100
Washington D.C.	46.15	4393	1372
Wilmington	32.40	965	106
United States	32.95	35317	3656

distribution to become more similar to that of white men, than would black men. On the basis of this index, we cannot, however, make any qualitative judgments as to which group is "better" or "worse" off in terms of occupational structures or occupational segregation. There are numerous reasons as to why the occupational structures of women may be more dissimilar to that of men than black males relative to white men. A partial list of these reasons may include gender differences in tastes for certain jobs, tastes with respect to labor force attachment, levels and types of skills, and levels of job discrimination.

Avoiding any type of qualitative judgments, we can, however, see how the index varies across SMSA's. This is shown in Table 5.11 for black/white male index

Table 5.8 1980 Black Male/White Male Occupational Segregation Index by SMSA			
SMSA	Index of Dissimilarity	Sample Size White Men	Sample Size Black Men
Akron	31.10	1419	103
Atlanta	31.95	3626	887
Baltimore	32.40	3752	958
Baton Rouge	33.20	834	228
Beaumont	32.70	721	146
Birmingham	33.50	1397	388
Boston	19.35	5560	240
Buffalo	25.05	2458	240
Charleston	31.05	595	200
Charlotte	30.85	1200	252
Chicago	29.75	12704	2254
Cincinnati	32.25	2565	309
Cleveland	34.80	3671	580
Columbia	35.20	611	207
Columbus	25.25	2150	226
Dallas/Ft. Worth	36.85	5790	769
Dayton	24.75	1552	158

	Table 5.8		
	1980 Black Male/White Male Occupational Segregation Index by SMSA		
SMSA	Index of Dissimilarity	Sample Size White Men	Sample Size Black Men
Detroit	29.25	8070	1505
Flint	27.00	997	134
Ft. Lauderdale	34.10	1776	193
Gary	29.40	1262	227
Greensboro	29.85	1389	254
Hartford	31.60	1530	110
Houston	35.80	5622	1043
Indianapolis	29.00	2391	296
Jackson	36.80	462	179
Jacksonville	36.90	1192	226
Kansas City	27.90	2655	296
Louisville	20.45	1854	187
LA/Long Beach	24.40	11603	1644
Memphis	42.10	1064	519
Miami	31.15	2543	490
Milwaukee	33.95	1988	245
Mobile	34.55	712	208
Nashville	28.55	1615	241
Nassau/Suffolk	26.45	5454	274
New Orleans	32.80	1834	591
Newport News	29.05	520	184

	Table 5.8		
	1980 Black Male/White Male Occupational Segregation Index by SMSA		
SMSA	Index of Dissimilarity	Sample Size White Men	Sample Size Black Men
New York	27.30	13515	3091
Newark	30.20	3566	728
Norfolk	34.70	787	254
Orlando	32.95	1314	127
Philadelphia	30.90	8248	1356
Pittsburgh	27.70	4743	265
Richmond	44.15	1120	344
Rochester	31.00	2012	125
St. Louis	30.30	4471	620
San Antonio	30.85	1612	114
San Diego	25.25	2893	145
San Francisco	28.90	5480	692
Shreveport	36.90	535	169
Tampa/St. Pete	30.65	2483	241
Toledo	25.60	1622	116
Washington D.C.	32.90	4910	1642
Wilmington	30.10	806	118
United States	29,35	40357	4250

SMSA	Index of Dissimilarity (S)	Sample Size Men	Sample Size Women
	Table 5.9 1970 White Male/White Female Occupational Segregation Index		
Akron	53.20	1395	877
Atlanta	46.95	2429	1905
Baltimore	44.65	3457	2411
Baton Rouge	54.75	410	253
Beaumont	61.25	526	279
Birmingham	52.90	1109	761
Boston	42.45	7204	5737
Buffalo	49.35	2640	1726
Charleston	49.30	351	286
Charlotte	53.80	692	562
Chicago	43.45	12848	8965
Cincinnati	45.50	2537	1696
Cleveland	47.95	3931	2601
Columbia	49.30	443	359
Columbus	46.70	1626	1270
Dallas/Ft. Worth	44.95	4417	3329
Dayton	50.90	1652	1085
Detroit	49.75	7620	4664
Flint	54.00	951	570
Ft. Lauderdale	48.80	1007	816

SMSA	Index of Dissimilarity (S)	Sample Size Men	Sample Size Women
	Table 5.9		
	1970 White Male/White Female Occupational Segregation Index		
Gary	54.90	1209	631
Greensboro	48.20	1098	915
Hartford	42.35	1729	1295
Houston	49.60	3659	2412
Indianapolis	44.35	2129	1575
Jackson	52.65	308	269
Jacksonville	51.15	818	628
Kansas City	45.55	2404	1901
Louisville	45.65	1565	1105
LA/Long Beach	41.50	13144	9623
Memphis	44.25	1012	798
Miami	47.00	2146	1771
Milwaukee	46.30	2816	2090
Mobile	47.35	539	347
Nashville	46.35	973	799
Nassau/Suffolk	46.40	5074	3155
New Orleans	49.50	1510	1016
Newport News	47.00	423	327
New York	40.55	15381	11464
Newark	43.75	3325	2278

	Table 5.9		
	1970 White Male/White Female Occupational Segregation Index		
SMSA	Index of Dissimilarity (S)	Sample Size Men	Sample Size Women
Norfolk	50.10	834	680
Orlando	50.40	728	546
Philadelphia	40.20	6565	4588
Pittsburgh	54.80	4892	2814
Richmond	45.90	886	687
Rochester	42.50	1733	1258
St. Louis	47.70	4250	2950
San Antonio	46.70	1313	1019
San Diego	43.10	2076	1648
San Francisco	43.95	5725	4181
Shreveport	44.00	380	271
Tampa/St. Pete	48.40	1502	1233
Toledo	51.50	1346	905
Washington D.C.	45.35	4393	3577
Wilmington	49.10	965	598
United States	44.15	35317	25819

Table 5.10			
1980 White Male/White Female Occupational Segregation Index			
SMSA	Index of Dissimilarity (S)	Sample Size Men	Sample Size Women
Akron	46.90	1419	987
Atlanta	38.20	3626	3039
Baltimore	37.85	3752	2855
Baton Rouge	49.20	834	545
Beaumont	55.90	721	418
Birmingham	49.50	1397	1024
Boston	33.95	5560	4713
Buffalo	44.25	2458	1849
Charleston	44.80	595	489
Charlotte	40.35	1200	1049
Chicago	38.35	12704	9840
Cincinnati	41.30	2565	1903
Cleveland	42.50	3671	2752
Columbia	39.05	611	572
Columbus	39.75	2150	1738
Dallas/Ft. Worth	37.10	5790	4730
Dayton	42.85	1552	1279
Detroit	44.50	8070	5726
Flint	47.85	997	706
Ft. Lauderdale	38.85	1776	1555
Gary	53.95	1262	791

	Table 5.10		
	1980 White Male/White Female Occupational Segregation Index		
SMSA	Index of Dissimilarity (S)	Sample Size Men	Sample Size Women
Greensboro	36.70	1389	1219
Hartford	37.00	1530	1261
Houston	44.00	5622	4070
Indianapolis	42.95	2391	1896
Jackson	44.80	462	401
Jacksonville	44.05	1192	1021
Kansas City	37.05	2655	2220
Louisville	44.30	1854	1426
LA/Long Beach	34.00	11603	9106
Memphis	41.45	1064	898
Miami	35.90	2543	2269
Milwaukee	41.35	1988	2363
Mobile	47.40	712	516
Nashville	36.45	1615	1369
Nassau/Suffolk	36.05	5454	3913
New Orleans	44.90	1834	1264
Newport News	40.40	520	439
New York	33.15	13515	10885
Newark	38.20	3566	2712
Norfolk	39.00	787	728
Orlando	35.70	1314	1099
Philadelphia	38.50	8248	6342

	Table 5.10 1980 White Male/White Female Occupational Segregation Index		
SMSA	Index of Dissimilarity (S)	Sample Size Men	Sample Size Women
Pittsburgh	47.10	4743	3250
Richmond	43.00	1120	892
Rochester	36.95	2012	1571
St. Louis	42.85	4471	3451
San Antonio	39.10	1612	1373
San Diego	34.75	2893	2335
San Francisco	33.20	5480	4506
Shreveport	39.00	535	430
Tampa/St. Pete	37.35	2483	2232
Toledo	49.40	1622	1188
Washington D.C.	33.05	4910	4224
Wilmington	42.55	806	594
United States	38.60	40357	32490

and in Table 5.12 for the white male/female index. Having calculated the index in both 1970 and 1980 for each SMSA, we can now determine the 10-year change in each SMSA. Actual 10-year SMSA changes in the index of dissimilarity, along with corresponding percentage changes in the index, are reported in Table 5.13 for black men and Table 5.14 for white women. The next section presents those local labor market conditions that are hypothesized to influence the relative occupational distribution of women and blacks.

Table 5.11				
1970 and 1980 Black/White Male Occupational Segregation Index:				
SMSA's Ranked in Descending Order				

1970		1980	
SMSA	Index of Dissimilarity	SMSA	Index of Dissimilarity
Jackson	51.65	Richmond	44.15
Ft. Lauderdale	48.10	Memphis	42.10
Richmond	47.95	Jacksonville	36.90
Shreveport	47.75	Shreveport	36.90
Charlotte	47.70	Dallas/Ft. Worth	36.85
Columbia	47.05	Jackson	36.80
Norfolk	47.05	Houston	35.80
Miami	46.75	Columbia	35.20
WashingtonD.C	46.15	Cleveland	34.80
Beaumont	45.10	Norfolk	34.70
Baton Rouge	44.90	Mobile	34.55
Jacksonville	43.95	Ft. Lauderdale	34.10
Dallas/Ft. Worth	43.90	Milwaukee	33.95
Tampa/St. Pete	43.65	Birmingham	33.50
Memphis	43.30	Baton Rouge	33.20
Atlanta	43.05	Orlando	32.95
Mobile	43.05	Washington D.C.	32.90
Orlando	42.45	New Orleans	32.80
New Orleans	42.10	Beaumont	32.70

Table 5.11		
1970 and 1980 Black/White Male Occupational Segregation Index: SMSA's Ranked in Descending Order			
1970		1980	
SMSA	Index of Dissimilarity	SMSA	Index of Dissimilarity
Newport News	39.75	Baltimore	32.40
Houston	39.30	Cincinnati	32.25
St. Louis	38.95	Atlanta	31.95
Akron	38.65	Hartford	31.60
Newark	38.50	Miami	31.15
Charleston	38.45	Akron	31.10
Nashville	38.45	Charleston	31.05
Birmingham	38.35	Rochester	31.00
Rochester	38.10	Philadelphia	30.90
Greensboro	37.35	San Antonio	30.85
Baltimore	37.20	Charlotte	30.85
Buffalo	36.35	Tampa/St. Pete	30.65
Detroit	35.20	St. Louis	30.30
Nassau/Suffolk	35.70	Newark	30.20
Milwaukee	34.15	Wilmington	30.10
Cleveland	34.00	Greensboro	29.85
San Diego	33.95	Chicago	29.75
Toledo	33.95	Gary	29.40
Kansas City	33.75	*United States	29.35

Table 5.11			
1970 and 1980 Black/White Male Occupational Segregation Index: SMSA's Ranked in Descending Order			
1970		1980	
SMSA	Index of Dissimilarity	SMSA	Index of Dissimilarity
Columbus	33.60	Detroit	29.35
Chicago	33.20	Newport News	29.05
*United States	32.95	Indianapolis	29.00
Hartford	32.65	San Francisco	28.90
Wilmington	32.40	Nashville	28.55
Cincinnati	32.15	Kansas City	27.90
San Francisco	31.95	Pittsburgh	27.70
Boston	30.45	New York	27.30
Philadelphia	30.45	Flint	27.00
Indianapolis	30.10	Nassau/Suffolk	26.45
Flint	30.05	Toledo	25.60
Louisville	29.20	Columbus	25.25
Pittsburgh	28.40	San Diego	25.25
LA/Long Beach	28.25	Buffalo	25.05
San Antonio	27.80	Dayton	24.75
Dayton	26.15	LA/Long Beach	24.40
New York	24.85	Louisville	20.45
Gary	24.60	Boston	19.35

Table 5.12			
1970 and 1980 White Female/Male Occupational Segregation Index: SMSA's Ranked in Descending Order			
1970		1980	
SMSA	Index of Dissimilarity	SMSA	Index of Dissimilarity
Beaumont	61.25	Beaumont	55.90
Gary	54.90	Gary	53.95
Pittsburgh	54.80	Birmingham	49.50
Baton Rouge	54.75	Toledo	49.40
Flint	54.00	Baton Rouge	49.20
Charlotte	53.80	Flint	47.85
Akron	53.20	Mobile	47.40
Birmingham	52.90	Pittsburgh	47.10
Jackson	52.65	Akron	46.90
Toledo	51.50	New Orleans	44.90
Jacksonville	51.15	Jackson	44.80
Dayton	50.90	Charleston	44.80
Orlando	50.40	Detroit	44.50
Norfolk	50.10	Louisville	44.30
Detroit	49.75	Buffalo	44.25
Houston	49.60	Jacksonville	44.05
New Orleans	49.50	Houston	44.00
Buffalo	49.35	Richmond	43.00
Charleston	49.30	Indianapolis	42.95

Table 5.12 1970 and 1980 White Female/Male Occupational Segregation Index: SMSA's Ranked in Descending Order			
1970		1980	
SMSA	Index of Dissimilarity	SMSA	Index of Dissimilarity
Columbia	49.30	Dayton	42.85
Wilmington	49.10	St. Louis	42.85
Ft. Lauderdale	48.80	Wilmington	42.55
Tampa/St. Pete	48.40	Cleveland	42.50
Greensboro	48.20	Memphis	41.45
Cleveland	47.95	Milwaukee	41.35
St. Louis	47.70	Cincinnati	41.30
Mobile	47.35	Newport News	40.40
Newport News	47.00	Charlotte	40.35
Miami	47.00	Columbus	39.75
Atlanta	46.95	San Antonio	39.10
Columbus	46.70	Columbia	39.05
San Antonio	46.70	Shreveport	39.00
Nassau/Suffolk	46.40	Norfolk	39.00
Nashville	46.35	Ft. Lauderdale	38.85
Milwaukee	46.30	*United States	38.60
Richmond	45.90	Philadelphia	38.50
Louisville	45.65	Chicago	38.35
Kansas City	45.55	Newark	38.20

Table 5.12			
1970 and 1980 White Female/Male Occupational Segregation Index: SMSA's Ranked in Descending Order			
1970		1980	
SMSA	Index of Dissimilarity	SMSA	Index of Dissimilarity
Cincinnati	45.50	Atlanta	38.20
Washington D.C.	45.35	Baltimore	37.85
Dallas/Ft. Worth	44.95	Tampa/St. Pete	37.35
Baltimore	44.65	Dallas/Ft. Worth	37.10
Indianapolis	44.35	Kansas City	37.05
Memphis	44.25	Hartford	37.00
*United States	44.15	Rochester	36.95
Shreveport	44.00	Greensboro	36.70
San Francisco	43.95	Nashville	36.45
Newark	43.75	Nassau/Suffolk	36.05
Chicago	43.45	Miami	35.90
San Diego	43.10	Orlando	35.70
Rochester	42.50	San Diego	34.75
Boston	42.45	LA/Long Beach	34.00
Hartford	42.35	Boston	33.95
LA/Long Beach	41.50	San Francisco	33.20
New York	40.55	New York	33.15
Philadelphia	40.20	Washington D.C.	33.05

	Table 5.13	
	1970-1980 Change in the Black/White Male Index of Dissimilarity of SMSA	
SMSA	Actual Change	Percentage Change
Akron	-7.55	-19.534
Atlanta	-11.10	-25.784
Baltimore	-4.80	-12.903
Baton Rouge	-11.70	-26.058
Beaumont	-12.40	-27.494
Birmingham	-4.85	-12.647
Boston	-11.10	-36.453
Buffalo	-11.30	-31.087
Charleston	-7.40	-19.246
Charlotte	-16.85	-35.325
Chicago	-3.45	-10.392
Cincinnati	0.10	0.311
Cleveland	0.80	2.353
Columbia	-11.85	-25.186
Columbus	-8.35	-24.851
Dallas/Ft. Worth	-7.05	-16.059
Dayton	-1.40	-534
Detroit	-6.95	-19.199
Flint	-3.05	-10.150

Table 5.13		
1970-1980 Change in the Black/White Male Index of Dissimilarity of SMSA		
SMSA	Actual Change	Percentage Change
Ft. Lauderdale	-14.00	-29.106
Gary	4.80	19.512
Greensboro	-7.50	-20.080
Hartford	-1.05	-3.216
Houston	-3.50	-8.906
Indianapolis	-1.10	-3.654
Jackson	-14.85	-28.751
Jacksonville	-7.05	-16.041
Kansas City	-5.85	-17.333
Louisville	-8.75	-29.966
LA/Long Beach	-3.85	-13.628
Memphis	-1.20	-2.771
Miami	-15.60	-33.369
Milwaukee	-0.20	-0.586
Mobile	-8.50	-19.744
Nashville	-9.90	-25.748
Nassau/Suffolk	-9.25	-25.910
New Orleans	-9.30	-22.090

Table 5.13 1970-1980 Change in the Black/White Male Index of Dissimilarity of SMSA		
SMSA	Actual Change	Percentage Change
Newport News	-10.70	-26.918
New York	2.45	9.859
Newark	-8.30	-21.558
Norfolk	-12.35	-26.249
Orlando	-9.50	-22.379
Philadelphia	0.45	1.478
Pittsburgh	-0.70	-2.465
Richmond	-3.80	-7.925
Rochester	-7.10	-18.635
St. Louis	-8.65	-22.208
San Antonio	3.05	10.971
San Diego	-8.70	-25.626
San Francisco	-3.00	-9.390
Shreveport	-10.85	-22.723
Tampa/St. Pete	-13.00	-29.782
Toledo	-8.35	-24.595
Washington D.C.	-13.25	-28.711
Wilmington	-2.30	-7.099
United States	-3.60	-10.926

Table 5.14		
1970-1980 Change in the White Male/Female Index of Dissimilarity by SMSA		
SMSA	Actual Change	Percentage Change
Akron	-6.30	-11.842
Atlanta	-8.75	-18.637
Baltimore	-6.80	-15.230
Baton Rouge	-5.555	-10.137
Beaumont	-5.35	-8.735
Birmingham	-3.40	-6.427
Boston	-8.50	-20.024
Buffalo	-5.10	-10.334
Charleston	-4.50	-9.128
Charlotte	-13.45	-25.000
Chicago	-5.10	-11.738
Cincinnati	-4.20	-9.231
Cleveland	-5.45	-11.738
Columbia	-10.25	-20.791
Columbus	-6.95	-14.882
Dallas/Ft. Worth	-7.85	-17.464
Dayton	-8.05	-15.815
Detroit	-5.25	-10.553
Flint	-6.15	-11.389
Ft. Lauderdale	-9.95	-20.389

Table 5.14 1970-1980 Change in the White Male/Female Index of Dissimilarity by SMSA		
SMSA	Actual Change	Percentage Change
Gary	-0.95	-1.730
Greensboro	-11.50	-23.859
Hartford	-5.35	-12.633
Houston	-5.60	-11.290
Indianapolis	-1.40	-3.157
Jackson	-7.85	-14.910
Jacksonville	-7.10	-13.881
Kansas City	-8.50	-18.661
Louisville	-1.35	-2.957
LA/Long Beach	-7.50	-18.072
Memphis	-2.80	-6.328
Miami	-11.10	-23.617
Milwaukee	-4.95	-10.691
Mobile	0.05	0.106
Nashville	-9.90	-21.359
Nassau/Suffolk	-10.35	-22.306
New Orleans	-4.60	-9.293
Newport News	-6.60	-14.043
New York	-7.40	-18.249
Newark	-5.55	-12.686
Norfolk	-11.10	-22.156
Orlando	-14.70	-29.167

Table 5.14 1970-1980 Change in the White Male/Female Index of Dissimilarity by SMSA		
SMSA	Actual Change	Percentage Change
Philadelphia	-1.70	-4.229
Pittsburgh	-7.70	-14.051
Richmond	-2.90	-6.318
Rochester	-5.55	-13.059
St. Louis	-4.85	-10.168
San Antonio	-7.60	-16.274
San Diego	-8.35	-19.374
San Francisco	-10.75	-24.460
Shreveport	-5.00	-11.364
Tampa/St. Pete	-11.05	-22.831
Toledo	-2.10	-4.078
Washington D.C.	-12.30	-27.122
Wilmington	-6.55	-13.340
United States	-5.55	-12.571

AGGREGATE MODEL

This section employs the index of dissimilarity from to assess the possible relationship between changes in local conditions and changes in the relative job distribution of women and blacks. As before, the term "minority" will refer to both black males and women.

Local Labor Market Conditions. A vector of measurable characteristics is again specified as serving as a proxy for conditions in a particular labor market. The following variables are proposed as influencing the relative occupational distributions of blacks and women.

The white male unemployment rate is proffered as the unemployment rate of the preferred group. Assuming discrimination exists in the labor market, a reduction in the white male unemployment rate signals that competition for jobs has changed such that employers find it more difficult to hire the preferred group, ceteris paribus. Minority workers who might not have been hired or promoted prior to this change (due to discrimination) may now have job opportunities available to them that previously had been reserved only for the preferred group (see Chapter III). If these workers now have more of the same job opportunities as the preferred group, we would expect their occupational distribution to become more similar to that of the preferred group, all else constant. Therefore, it is hypothesized that a reduction in the white male unemployment rate is associated with a reduction in the index of dissimilarity between the preferred and the minority group, implying that the two job distributions have become more similar.

A change in the unionization rate of a labor market may have a positive or a negative impact on the relative occupational distribution of the minority group. If minorities benefit more from union membership than their white male counterparts (Hirsch and Addison 1986), an increase in the unionization rate results in opportunities that are more similar to those of white males. This would cause the two job distributions to become more similar, thereby reducing the index of dissimilarity. On the other hand, if unions themselves are one of the discriminating agents (Ashenfelter 1972), then an increase in the unionization rate might cause the two occupational distributions to become more dissimilar. Given these two possibilities, we, therefore, choose not to hypothesize a priori the direction of the relationship between a change in the SMSA's unionization rate and the index of dissimilarity.

On average, white men have attained higher educational levels than their comparable minority counterparts--this is especially true for the traditionally higher paying occupations such as professional, managerial and technical professions (see Census 1983a). If the educational levels of minorities were to rise and approach that of white men, it is reasonable to expect that the occupational distributions of minority workers should become more similar to that of white men, ceteris paribus. To test this, we calculate the change in the proportion of the minority working age population possessing at least a high school diploma. Thus, we expected a negative relationship between this variable and the index of dissimilarity.

A change in the labor force participation rate of the minority group in an SMSA is again offered as a proxy for a change in the relative supply of that minority group. Assuming discrimination exists in the labor market, an increase in the relative supply of the minority group would tend to "crowd" these workers into those occupations where minorities are already prevalent (for a discussion of the "crowding hypothesis" see Cain 1976). If employers tend to exclude minority workers from certain jobs, then an increase in the relative supply of the minority group would tend to be associated with an increase in the index of dissimilarity, as more of the minority workers obtain jobs in those occupations in which they are over represented relative to white males (Beller 1982).

Changes in the variables construction employment, manufacturing employment, and population again serve as proxies for changes in the relative demand for labor (see Chapter IV). Increases in these variables would reflect expansionary forces in an SMSA and would approximate an increase in labor demand for that SMSA. It is hypothesized that increases in the relative demand for labor would allow minority workers access to those jobs that were previously reserved for white males as employers fill those new jobs created by the increase in labor demand. Therefore, an increase in the variables construction employment, manufacturing employment, and population are expected to be associated with reductions in the index of dissimilarity, ceteris paribus.

Changes in antipoverty transfer programs may also be related to changes in the relative occupational structures of workers. If these programs become more liberal, workers may opt for these programs in lieu of labor market participation. If workers from the preferred and the minority groups are affected differently this would cause the index of dissimilarity to change. For example, if more of the highly able workers from the minority group dropped out of the labor force (relative to the preferred group) this may cause the two occupational distributions to diverge from one another. If, on the other hand, more of the less-able workers from the minority group withdrew from the labor force, then they may be withdrawing from occupations where they were already over represented (relative to white males). This would cause the two job distributions to possibly become more similar, ceteris paribus. The variables number of individuals receiving AFDC and average AFDC family payments are used to proxy antipoverty programs in this analysis (see Chapter IV). Given these possibilities, no a priori hypothesis is made concerning the expected relationship between changes in our proxies for welfare programs and the index of dissimilarity..

Table 5.15 summarizes the expected sign on the relationship between the proffered variables and the associated change in the index of dissimilarity.

Table 5.15 Hypothesized Effects of Changes in Local Labor Market Variables on the Index of Dissimilarity	
(an increase in the) Local Labor Market Variable	Hypothesized Relationship to the index (S)
White male unemployment rate	+
Labor force participation rate of black males	+
Labor force participation rate of white females	+
Percentage of the labor force unionized	?
Proportion of the black working age population having at least a high school diploma	-
Proportion of the female working age population having at least a high school diploma	-
Construction employment	-
Manufacturing employment	-
Population	-
Number of individuals receiving AFDC	?
Average AFDC payment per family	?

Empirical Results. The discussion in the previous section outlined the local labor market variables that are hypothesized to relate to the relative occupational distribution of women and blacks. In Chapter III, a general form of an aggregate model was specified that would test the various propositions from the previous section. Based on equation (3–14), the general form of the model can be expressed as:

(3-14) $\Delta S_j = \tau_o + \tau_1 \Delta \alpha_{1j} + \tau_2 \Delta \alpha_{2j} + \ldots + \tau_k \Delta \alpha_{kj} + \epsilon.$

Where j represents the jth SMSA, $\Delta \alpha_{1j}$, $\Delta \alpha_{2j}$, . . ., $\Delta \alpha_{kj}$ represent the percentage change in the k local labor market variables, τ_0, τ_1, τ_2, . . ., $_k$ are the parameters to be estimated. The dependent variable, Δs_j, is the percentage change in the index of dissimilarity in the Jth SMSA. Multivariate regression techniques are used to estimate the parameters in equation (3–14). The signs on the ordinary least squares estimates will provide an indication of the direction of the association between the percentage change in the local labor market variable and the percentage change in the index of dissimilarity.

The estimates of equation (3–14) for black males are given in the first column of Table 5.16. At conventional levels of significance, the significant coefficients are: the percentage change in the labor force participation rate of black males; the percentage change in the population of an SMSA; and the percentage change in the number of individuals receiving AFDC. The negative sign on the population coefficient implies that labor markets characterized by population growth are associated with reductions in the index of dissimilarity. The coefficients for construction and manufacturing employment (although insignificant) suggest; however, that employment increases in these industries are associated with greater occupational dissimilarities between black and white males.

The coefficient for the percentage change in the unionization rate has a negative sign associated with it, although it is not significant. Separate estimates were obtained using only state unionization data, and only those SMSA's for which union data was available. There were, however, no significant differences between any of the models. The coefficient on the percentage change in the white male unemployment rate does have the hypothesized sign, yet it is not significant in explaining changes in the index of dissimilarity.

The coefficient on the AFDC variables suggest that more liberal antipoverty programs are associated with greater similarities between the occupational distributions of white and black men. This result lends support to the notion that more generous antipoverty programs may lead lower skilled black men to drop out of the labor force in favor of non-market activities (see Butler and Heckman 1977; Brown 1984; Smith and Welch 1989). If these lower skilled individuals are leaving the labor force, it would then be reasonable to expect the occupational distributions of the remaining black men to become more similar to those of white men. The negative sign on the AFDC coefficients supports this hypothesis.

Table 5.16 Estimated Aggregate Equation Black/White Males			
Dependent Variable:	Percentage Change in the Index of Dissimilarity between Black & White Males (Standard Error in Parentheses)		
Exogenous Variable	Estimated Coefficient	Estimated Coefficient	Estimated Coefficient
Constant	-21.401* (9.989)	-12.659 (9.755)	-13.581 (11.282)
%CHG WHITE MALE UNEMPLOYMENT RATE	0.037 (0.045)	0.024 (0.046)	0.079** (0.044)
5CHG BLACK MALE LABOR FORCE PARTICIPATION RATE	-1.284* (0.624)		
%CHG SMSA UNION RATE	-0.067 (0.097)	0.020 (0.100)	-0.014 (0.102)
%CHG IN PROPORTION OF BLACK MALES W/ HIGH SCHOOL DIPLOMA	0.113 (0.127)	-0.042 (0.122)	-0.098 (0.119)
%CHG IN SMSA POPULATION	-0.391* (0.186)	-0.284*** (0.191)	

Table 5.16
Estimated Aggregate Equation Black/White Males

Dependent Variable: Percentage Change in the Index of
                           Dissimilarity between Black & White Males
                           (Standard Error in Parentheses)

Exogenous Variable	Estimated Coefficient	Estimated Coefficient	Estimated Coefficient
%CHG IN CONSTRUCTION EMPLOYMENT	0.087 (0.164)	-0.010 (0.162)	-0.054 (0.184)
%CHG IN MANUFACTURING EMPLOYMENT	0.124 (0.289)	-0.186 (0.286)	-0.233 (0.281)
%CHG IN # INDIVIDUALS RECEIVING AFDC	-0.179* (0.082)		-0.173* (0.086)
%CHG IN AVERAGE FAMILY AFDC PAYMENTS	-0.076 (0..079)		-0.066 (0.816)
%CHG IN BLACK SMSA POPULATION			0.014 (0.258)
R^2	0.3295	0.1691	0.2156

*Significant at the 5% level.
**Significant at the 10% level.
***Significant at the 15% level.

The coefficient on the percentage change in labor force participation rates of black men is, however, inconsistent with this hypothesis. In the 55 SMSA's used in this study, 35 experienced reductions in the labor force participation of their black male working age population over the ten year period, a finding which is consistent with that of other researchers (e.g., Smith and Welch 1989). If this decline in labor force participation rates was due to lower skilled blacks dropping out of the labor force, we would expect a positive coefficient in the aggregate model. Instead we find the opposite to be true. This finding might suggest that it is higher skilled blacks leaving the labor force, rather than lower skilled blacks. If higher skilled black workers were to leave the labor force, then we would expect the occupational distribution of the remaining black workers to become more dissimilar to that of white males. The significantly negative coefficient on the black male labor force participation rate is puzzling given the results of the AFDC coefficient.

Table 5.17			
Estimated Aggregate Equation White Male/Female			
Dependent Variable:	Percentage Change in the Index of Dissimilarity between White Males and White Females (Standard Error in Parentheses)		
Exogenous Variable	Estimated Coefficient	Estimated Coefficient	Estimated Coefficient
Constant	-21.872* (6.390)	-24.098* (3.716)	_24.318* (3.835)
%CHG WHITE MALE UNEMPLOYMENT RATE	0.031** (0.017)	0.032** (0.017)	0.032** (0.017)
% CHG FEMALE LABOR FORCE PART. RATE	-0.127 (0.218)		
% CHG SMSA UNION RATE	-0.048 (0.038)	-0.045 (0.355)	-0.046 (0.036)
% CHG IN PROPORTION OF FEMALES W/ HIGH SCHOOL DIPLOMA	0.289** (0.153)	0.285* (0.144)	0.294* (0.149)

Table 5.17 Estimated Aggregate Equation White Male/Female			
Dependent Variable:	Percentage Change in the Index of Dissimilarity between White Males and White Females (Standard Error in Parentheses)		
Exogenous Variable	Estimated Coefficient	Estimated Coefficient	Estimated Coefficient
% CHG IN SMSA POPULATION	-0.089 (0.068)	0.094** (0.595)	0.088 (0.642)
% CHG IN CONSTRUCTION EMPLOYMENT	0.125** (0.068)	0.111** (0.063)	0.115** (0.065)
% CHG IN MANUFACTURING EMPLOYMENT	0.124 (0.111)	-0.120 (0.105)	0.113 (0.110)
% CHG IN # INDIVIDUALS RECEIVING AFDC	0.007 (0.031)		
% CHG IN AVERAGE AFDC PAYMENTS	0.006 (0.031)		
% CHG IN # FAMILIES BELOW THE POVERTY LEVEL			0.012 (0.044)
R^2	0.4286	0.4222	0.4231
*Significant at the 5% level. ** Significant at the 10% level. ***Significant at the 15% level.			

Alternative specifications of the aggregate model are presented in the second and third columns of Table 5.16. The second model, which omits the labor force participation and AFDC variables, does a poor job explaining variations in changes of the index of dissimilarity. In the third model, the black male labor force participation rate is omitted and instead, changes in the black population of an SMSA is used as proxy for the relative supply of black men. The significant coefficients in this model are the percentage change in the white male unemployment rate (which has the hypothesized sign), and the percentage change in the number of individuals receiving AFDC (which again has a negative sign). The coefficient on the SMSA black population, while having the hypothesized sign, is insignificant.

For women, the results of the aggregate model are presented in the first column in Table 5.17. At conventional levels, the coefficients on the following variables are significant: the percentage change in the white male unemployment rate; the percentage change in the proportion of women with at least a high school diploma and the percentage change in construction employment. The coefficients on the percentage change in the white male unemployment rate has the hypothesized sign, as do the coefficients on the percentage change in population and manufacturing employment. It appears that as the white male unemployment rate rises, the occupational attainment of women becomes more dissimilar to that of men.

The coefficient on the labor force participation variable has an opposite sign of what is hypothesized, and is insignificant. Between 1970 and 1980, the labor force participation rate of women rose in all 55 SMSA's. It seems that with the large increase in the labor force participation of women during the 1970's, that the occupational distributions of women have become more similar to that of men. A few economists have attributed this narrowing of the occupational distributions to the success of programs such as affirmative action and equal employment opportunity legislation (see e.g., Beller 1982, 1985; Gunderson 1989). Empirical studies conducted in this area do not, however, unilaterally support the idea that anti-discrimination programs. Have been a "resounding success" with respect to the relative economic status of women (Gunderson 1989, p. 61).

The sign on the percentage change in the proportion of women with at least a high school diploma also has the opposite sign of what is hypothesized. This finding is consistent with the hypothesis proffered by some economists (e.g., Blau and Ferber 1992) that "while women have similar levels of education to men, the type of education women acquire is often not as oriented towards gaining skills that are rewarded in the labor market" (Gunderson 1989, p.52). If women are pursuing types of education that are not as marketable as education pursued by men, this would lead to a divergence in the two occupational distributions. Alternative specifications are reported in the second and third columns of Table 5.17, with results similar to those reported in column one.

The results of the aggregate models presented in this section do not overwhelmingly support the notion that changes in local labor market conditions are related to the relative occupational attainment of women and black men.

SUMMARY

The purpose of this chapter was to develop a model that would allow us to test empirically whether changes in the relative occupational structures of white women and black men are systematically related to changing conditions in a labor market. Our analysis provides limited support for using an SMSA to represent a local occupational labor market. A comparison of the occupational distributions of women and blacks with those of their white male counterparts was accomplished by calculating an index of dissimilarity for each SMSA in 1970 and 1980. We then estimated an aggregate model that allowed us to test hypothetical relationships between changes in measurable attributes of local labor markets and the relative occupational structures of women and blacks. As with the wage model Chapter IV, the results presented in this chapter fail to provide convincing evidence of systematic relationships between changing attributes of a labor market and changes in the relative occupational attainment of women and blacks.

VI

Summary and Conclusions

Much of the empirical research on the relative economic status of women and blacks concentrates on how these groups fare relative to white males in the U.S. labor market. Many of these studies, however, have not examined explicitly whether the relative status of these groups varies across local labor markets or whether the relative status of these groups is systematically associated with economic attributes of a local labor market. This study investigates the effects that local labor market conditions have on the economic status of women and blacks relative to white men. Specifically, we investigate whether conventional estimates of wage and occupational discrimination vary across local labor markets and whether they are systematically related to changes in measurable attributes of those labor markets.

Chapter II summarizes the major works in the literature concerning labor market discrimination and the relative economic status of women and minorities. This chapter also discusses the conventional methods which economists employ to estimate empirically the existence and extent of differential labor market treatment (such as discrimination). This review of the literature indicates that many studies on the economic status of women and minorities assume that the U.S. may be viewed as a national labor market. Research by Hirsch, Hanushek, Topel, and others, however, suggest that the U.S. is composed of many distinct local labor markets.

In Chapter III, the link between the relative economic status of minorities and changes in labor market conditions is explored. Economists such as Shulman, Tobin, and McCall (among others) have raised the possibility that the economic status of minorities is linked to changing labor market conditions. For example, they contend that as labor market conditions tighten, the costs of discrimination to the firm increase. This implies that women and minorities may fare better with respect to wage and occupational opportunities as conditions in a labor market improve. Also in Chapter III, a model is formulated that allows us to empirically assess whether labor market conditions are related to conventional estimates of wage and occupational discrimination.

157

Chapters IV and V present the empirical specifications and results of the wage and occupational models. In Chapter IV, earnings models for white women, white men, and black men are specified based on the human capital approach of Mincer (1974) and others. These models are then estimated using data from the 1970 and 1980 U.S. Census of Population and Housing. Hypothesis tests espoused by Hirsch (1978) are employed in determining whether a national or local labor market (represented by an SMSA) is appropriate for use in this analysis. The results of these hypotheses tests lead us to reject the use of a national labor market and hence, would suggest that the wage structures of white males, black males, and white females differ across local labor markets. In addition, the earnings models in Chapter IV are used to assess if the observed race and gender earnings differences are due to differences in worker characteristics or to other factors such as discrimination. Estimates of the portion of the earnings differential not attributable to differences in productivity related characteristics are what analysts frequently interpret as upper bound estimates of wage discrimination. These estimates are calculated for each of 55 representative SMSA's for both 1970 and 1980, along with the corresponding 10-year change.

Also in Chapter IV, we specified an aggregate model to assess the possible relationship between changes in our estimates of discrimination and changes in labor market conditions. Using multivariate regression analysis, we regressed the 10-year change in our estimate of wage discrimination on the changes in labor market attributes (such as labor force participation patterns, unemployment rates, population trends, among others) for each SMSA. From the results of our models, it appears that there is no systematic association between changes in estimates of wage discrimination and changes in measurable labor market characteristics.

In Chapter V, a similar procedure is adopted in examining race and gender differences in occupational structures. The local (i.e., SMSA) occupational structures of women, black men, and white men are compared to a national distribution. The comparisons indicate that in some SMSA's, the occupational distribution of workers differs significantly from the corresponding national distribution. This suggests that occupational structures of workers may vary across local labor markets. In comparing the job distributions of women and blacks (relative to white men), we make use of the index of dissimilarity. This index is calculated for each SMSA in 1970 and 1980, along with the corresponding 10-year change.

As with the wage models, multivariate regression analysis was used to test whether changes in local labor market characteristics are related to changes in estimates of occupational segregation. The results of this analysis suggest that variations in changes in the index of dissimilarity are not explained very well by changes in measurable labor market characteristics.

In analyzing changes in estimated wage and occupational discrimination by race, changes in antipoverty programs (proxied in our analysis by Aid to Families with Dependent Children--AFDC) appear to be significant in both models. The percentage change in the number of individuals receiving AFDC in an SMSA is positively associated with changes in estimates of wage discrimination, yet negatively associated with changes in the index of dissimilarity.

In exploring the relationship between changes in estimates of wage and occupational discrimination against women and changes in local labor market characteristics, changes in the white male unemployment rate appear to be significant. The percentage change in the white male unemployment rate is positively associated with changes in the index of dissimilarity (which was hypothesized in our analysis) and negatively associated with changes in estimates of wage discrimination. This suggests that as the white male unemployment rate rises, the occupational distributions of men and women becomes more dissimilar, while the unexplained portion of the wage differential becomes smaller.

In general, the efficacy of the occupational model is superior to that of the wage model, yet neither gives overwhelming support to the notion that a systematic association exists between changes in local labor market characteristics and changes in conventional estimates of wage and occupational discrimination. There are several possibilities that may account for these findings. One possibility is that changes in labor market conditions, which affect the wages and occupations of workers, may generally affect all workers possessing similar skills. That is, if wages and occupations of equally productive white male and minority workers are affected in approximately the same way, changes in estimates of discrimination might be invariant to changes in local labor market conditions. Another possibility suggests that disparities across labor markets, which favors the economic status of one group over another, should equalize over time--a possibility supported by neoclassical theory. This interpretation suggests systematic differences in local labor market conditions which might favor wages or occupational distributions of minority (or female) workers are equalizing over the ten year period. This might also explain the failure of changes in local labor market conditions to explain changes in estimates of discrimination.

There are several areas in which future research may provide additional insight into the relationship between local labor markets and the relative economic status of women and blacks. First, our analysis may be employed to focus on the "raw" relative wage (i.e., the wage ratio) of minorities instead of conventional estimates of wage discrimination. This type of analysis would investigate if changes in wage ratios are affected by changes in aggregate local labor market conditions (e.g., the relative average level of education completed by each group, the relative average experience levels of each group, as well as other characteristics.

A second area of future research might incorporate sources of occupational disparities of workers and whether these sources are linked to local labor market conditions. Incorporating additional occupational categories might also provide further insight into the role of local labor market conditions and the relative occupational distributions of workers.

Further investigations in this area might also make use of different data sets and other minority groups (e.g., Hispanics, Asians, among others) to verify the results of this analysis. In addition, this type of analysis might benefit from the development of alternative data sets. Examples of the types of data that would aid our understanding of the role that local labor market conditions have on the relative economic status of minorities (and women) include: more disaggregated data on individual workers (for example, firm specific data) with detailed personnel records on worker qualifications; more detailed information on labor market attributes; and more consistent reporting of labor market attributes (rather than some characteristics being reported by SMSA, others by city, and yet others by country).

The results of the study suggest that the U.S. is composed of many distinct local labor markets and further suggest that the wage and occupational structures of workers vary across these labor markets. The role of local labor market conditions in explaining these different structures should remain a fruitful area for future research.

Notes

Chapter II

1.   The case of employee discrimination is explained by Arrow (1972) as it related to racial discrimination. If the wages for whites exceeds that for black, and white workers are willing to accept a lower wage to work only with whites:

> . . .A little reflection makes it obvious that if the wages required by whites for an all-white labor force are lower than black wages, total segregation for whites is optimum for the firm, while in the contrary case an all-black labor force is cheapest. We are, of course, still assuming equal productivity for the two races. At a general equilibrium with full employment of both types of labor, some firms must be segregated in one direction and some in the other. It would never pay a firm to have a mixed labor force, since they would have to raise the wages of their white workers above the level for an all-white option. The firms would also have to find the two types of segregation equally profitable; otherwise, they would all switch to one or the other. This requires that wages paid to whites in the all-white firms equal that paid to blacks in the all-black firms. There would be again no wage differentials. (Arrow 1972, p. 92).

2.   Becker and Arrow also consider the impact of customer discrimination (see Becker 1971 and Arrow 1972 for details).

3.   This restrictive assumption is relaxed later.

4.   Relaxing the assumption of perfect substitutes implies that workers marginal products will differ (i.e., $MP_A = Q'_A \neq MP_B = Q'_B$). In this case, employer discrimination is defined as:

$$MP_B/MP_A = d_B (W_B/W_A) \text{ (Butler 1982)}.$$

If $d_B > 1$, the firm acts as though they are paying more for B labor than they actually are. This can be extended to the case of equally productive workers where "we observe [B] being paid a lower wage than [A]" (Butler 1982, p. 606).

5.   A recent study by Shackett and Trapani (1987) examined market structure and earnings. The types of market structures they examined were regulated industries, nonprofit industries, private nonregulated industries and government sector. Using NLS cohort data, they find:

> . . .no significant differential by race attributable to market structure except for black women in nonprofit industries, the mean wage is larger for whites than for blacks in all structure categories. These differences in wages are thus partly attributable to differences in the mean level of productive characteristics of blacks and whites in our sample, as well as differing returns to these productive characteristics (pp. 528-529).

Thus, when testing for differences in discrimination by market structure, they find no significant difference in earnings differentials by race for males and for females, no significant difference except for black women in nonprofit industries (p. 529).

6.   Other explanations Blau discusses are the statistical discrimination model by Aigner and Cain and Arrow's "feedback model" (see Blau 1984, pp. 57-59 for details).

7.   From the wage equations it can be seen that low unemployment tends to be associated with higher wages for blacks while high unemployment tends to be associated with lower wages. Blinder did not, however, present means for the explanatory variables. Thus, it is not possible to discern the portion of the wage differential explained by each of the local labor market dummy variables.

8.   Blinder (1973) did, however, note that the results pertaining to local labor market conditions "ought to be discounted heavily since our dummy variables are very imperfect indices of local labor market conditions" (p. 449).

9.   The notion of sample selection bias and the implications it has on estimating earnings functions will be discussed in detail in Chapter IV.

10.   O'Neill found that among full-time working women, younger women tend to have increased their work experience, and that those women in the labor force tend to be staying longer, which

also increases work experience (p. S114). This may then account for the narrowing of the wage gap which has been observed since the mid-1070's.

11. Blinder (1973) did include dummy variables for local labor market conditions but, by his own admission, these are imperfect measures (see footnote 1). Also, by using these dummy variables, the same limitations apply that apply to using regional dummy variables.

12. In their study, Hyclak and Johnes (1987) explored the determinants of local full employment unemployment rates (FEUR) for 43 local labor markets in Pennsylvania. The local labor markets (delineated by the Pennsylvania Department of Labor) included 14 SMSAs and 29 non-metropolitan areas. Hyclak and Johnes found there was "substantial variation in the estimated FEURs across the local labor markets in the sample" (p. 198).

13. Often a single index number, called the index of dissimilarity, is used to make such comparisons. This index is discussed in greater detail later in this analysis.

Chapter III

1. To qualify this, Becker (1971) noted that the larger the number of workers from group B, the lower will be group B's wages. With a significantly large number of B workers, wages in this case may be slower to rise with improvements in the labor market, however, the direction of the wage change should be the same. This may imply a decline in wage discrimination (although less than in a market with proportionately fewer B workers).

2. This leads to the familiar indexing problem in wage decomposition analysis. One might just as well assume that in the absence of discrimination A workers would receive the same wage as B ceteris paribus, or that in the absence of discrimination a nondiscriminatory wage might lie somewhere between the two (see Cotton 1988); Reimers 1983). For the moment, I will follow Oaxaca's general method whereby the assumption outlined in the text is being followed.

3. Butler (1982, 1983) has offered a production function technique

as an alternative to the human capital approach. However, his technique requires specific information on production function parameters for a local labor market--information that is currently unavailable for a study encompassing a large number of local markets (Butler 1982, p. 613; 1983, pp. 978-983). Other alternative techniques (e.g., "reverse regression") have received attention in the literature (Kamalich and Polachek 1982). However, these techniques also suffer from substantial criticism (for a discussion of these techniques and criticisms see Blau 1984, pp. 62-65).

4.   Specification of Θ will come in the next Chapter.

Chapter IV

1.   The inverse of the Mills ratio (LAMBDA$_i$ = $f(Z_i \delta)$ / $F(Z_i \delta)$ where $f(\cdot)$ is the standard normal density function and $F(\cdot)$ is the standard normal distribution function (Heckman 1980, p. 214; Reimers 1983, p. 572).

2.   Here we adopt the standard technique of choosing the (presumably) nondiscriminated group, white males, as the reference group.

3.   This interpretation has been criticized by Butler (1982, 1983) and Jones (1983).

4.   To check the wage decomposition procedure, we performed a test whereby the unexplained earnings differential between white males in different SMSA's was calculated for 1980. The four SMSA's chosen were: Pittsburgh (used as the reference group); Milwaukee; Los Angeles; and Atlanta. The observed wage gap ranged (in logs) from -0.026 to 0.07. After correcting for selectivity bias, the wage gap (in logs) ranged from -0.006 to 0.068. Given the very small wage differences, any slight difference in the estimated coefficients had a magnified effect on the percentage of the wage difference unexplained by productivity-related characteristics. These estimates ranged from -529.39 percent to 153.70 percent.

5.   An experiment to check the impact of selectivity bias on our estimates of wage discrimination was conducted using a pooled model for 1980. In the pooled model the portion of the wage difference unexplained by worker characteristics was calculated

with and without correction for sample selection bias. A second model was specified where the characteristics of an SMSA in 1980 were introduced as explanatory variables in the wage equations. These wage equations were then estimates with and without correction for sample selection bias. Wage decomposition of these wage equations yielded the following percentages of the unexplained wage difference:

Black/White Males		
	Wage Equation Without SMSA Attributes	Wage Equation with SMSA Attributes
with sample selection correction	23.58	19.55
without sample selection correction	51.73	49.92

White Male/Female		
	Wage Equation Without SMSA Attributes	Wage Equation with SMSA Attributes
with sample selection correction	60.86	60.92
without sample selection correction	61.50	61.18

The sample selection procedure had no significant impact on wage discrimination estimates for women. For black men, however, the sample selection procedure did significantly impact our estimates.

6.   Chiswick was referring to highly able, highly motivated immigrant workers overcoming earnings discrimination. This argument may be extended to include highly able and highly motivated minority workers as well.

7.   The percentage change in the SMSA's union rate is only given for 33 of the SMSA's (Kokkelenberg and Sockell 1985; Freeman and Medoff 1979). If the SMSA union rate was not available, the percentage change in the state union rate was substituted. To check these results, separate models were estimated for the 33 SMSA's where union data was available, and again for all 55 SMSA's using the percentage change in state union rates as the union variable. There were, however, no significant differences between the models.

Bibliography

Addison, John T. And W. Stanley Siebert. 1979. *The Market for Labor: An Analytical Treatment.* Santa Monica: Goodyear Publishing Company.

Aiger, D.J. and G.C. Cain. 1977. "Statistical Theories of Discrimination in Labor Markets." *Industrial and Labor Relations Review* 12: 175-187.

Albelda, Randy P. 1986. "Occupational Segregation by Race and Gender, 1958-1981." *Industrial and Labor Relations Review* 39: 404-411.

Arrow, Kenneth J. 1972a. "Models of Job Discrimination." *Racial Discrimination in Economic Life.* Ed. Anthony H. Rascal. Lexington, MA: D.C. Heath and Co. 83-102/

Arrow, Kenneth J. 1972b. "Some Mathematical Models of Race in the Labor Market." *Racial Discrimination in Economic Life.* Ed. Anthony H. Pascal. Lexington, MA: D.D. Heath and Co. 187-204.

Arrow, Kenneth J. 1973. "The Theory of Discrimination." *Discrimination in Labor Markets.* Ed. Orley Ashenfelter and Albert Rees. Princeton: Princeton university Press. 3-33.

Ashenfelter, Orley. 1972. "Racial Discrimination and Trade Unionism." *Journal of Political Economy* 80.3: 435:464.

Becker, Gary S. 1971. *The Economics of Discrimination.* 2nd ed. Chicago: University of Chicago Press.

Becker, Gary S. 1975. *Human Capital.* 2nd ed. New York: National Bureau of Economic Research.

Behman, Sara. 1978. "Interstate Differentials in Wages and Unemployment." *Industrial Relations* 17.2: 168-188.

Beller, Andrea H. 1985. "Changes in the Sex Composition of U.S. Occupation, 1960-1981." *Journal of Human Resources* 20.2: 233-250.

Beller, Andrea H. 1982. "Occupational Segregation by Sex: Determinants and Changes." *Journal of Human Resources* 17:371-392.

Berger, Mark C. and Darrell, Glenn. 1986. "Selectivity Bias and Earnings Differences by Gender and Race." *Economics Letters* 21: 291-296.

Bergmann, Barbara R. 1974. "Occupational Segregation, Wages and Profits When Employers Discriminate by Race or Sex." *Eastern Economic Journal* 1.2: 103–110.

Bergmann, Barbara R. 1971. "The Effect on White Incomes of Discrimination in Employment," *Journal of Political Economy* 79: 294–313.

Blau, Francine D. 1984. "Discrimination Against Women: Theory and Evidence." *Labor Economics: Modern Views*. Ed. William Darity, Jr. Boston: Kluwer-Nijhoff Publishing. 53–89.

Blau, Francine D. and Andrea H. Beller. 1988. "Trends in Earnings Differentials by Gender, 1972–1981." *Industrial and Labor Relations Review* 41: 513–529.

Blau, Francine D. and Marianne A. Feber. 1986. *The Economics of Women, Men, and Work*. Englewood Cliffs, N.J.: Prentice-Hall.

Blaug, Mark. 1976. "The Empirical Status of Human Capital Theory: A Slightly Jaundiced Survey." *Journal of Economic Literature* 14: 827–855.

Blaug, Mark. 1980. *The Methodology of Economics*. Cambridge: Cambridge University Press.

Blinder, Alan S. 1973. "Wage Discrimination: Reduced Form and Structural Estimates." *Journal of Human Resources* 8: 436–455.

Blinder, Alan S. 1976. "On Dogmatism in Human Capital Theory." *Journal of Human Resources* 11: 8–22.

Brown, Charles. 1984. "Black-White Earnings Ratios Since the Civil Rights Act of 1964: The Importance of Labor Market Dropouts." *Quarterly Journal of Economics* :32–44.

Brown, Charles. 1982. "The Federal Attack on Labor Market Discrimination: The Mouse That Roared?" *Research in Labor Economics.* Ed. Ronald G. Ehrengerg. 5: 33–68.

Burris, Val and Amy Wharton. 1982. "Sex Segregation in The U.S. Labor Force." *Review of Radical Political Economics* 14: 43–56.

Butler, Richard J. 1982. "Estimating Wage Discrimination in the Labor Market." *Journal of Human Resources* 17: 606–621.

Butler, Richard J. 1983. "Direct Estimates of the Demand for the Race and Sex Discrimination." *Southern Economic Journal* 49: 975–990.

Butler, Richard and James Heckman. 1977. "The Government's Impact on the Labor Market Status of Black Americans: A Critical Review." *Equal Rights and Industrial Relations.* Ed. Leonard J. Hausman et. Al. Madison, WI: Industrial Relations Research Association. 235–281.

Cain, Glen G. 1976. "The Challenge of Segmented Labor Market Theories to Orthodox Theory: A Survey." *Journal of Economic Literature* 14: 1215–1257.

Carlson, Leonard A. and Caroline Swartz. 1988. "The Earnings of Women and Ethnic Minorities, 1959–1979." *Industrial and Labor Relations Review* 41.4: 530–546.

Chiplin, Brian. 1981. "An Alternative Approach to the Measurement of Sex Discrimination: An Illustration from University Entrance." *The Economic Journal* 91: 988–997.

Chiplin, Brian and P.J. Sloane. 1974. "Sexual Discrimination in the Labour Market." *British Journal of Industrial relations* 12.3: 371–403.

Chiplin, Brian and P.J. Sloane. 1976a. "Personal Characteristics and Sex Differentials in Professional Employment." *The Economic Journal* 86: 729–745.

Chiplin, Brian and P.J. Sloane. 1976b. "Male-Female Earnings Differences: A Further Analysis.: *British Journal of Industrial Relations* 14.1: 77–81.

Chiswick, Barry R. 1974. *Income Inequality* New York: National Bureau of Economic Research.

Chiswick, Barry R. 1978. "The Effect of Americanization on the Earnings of Foreign-born Men." *Journal of Political Economy* 86: 879–921.

Chiswick, Barry R. and June A. O'Neill. 1977. *Human Resources and Income Distribution.* New York: W.W. Norton and Company, Inc.

Corcoran, Mary and Greg J. Duncan. 1979. "Work History, Labor Force Attachment, and Earnings Differences between the Races and Sexes." *Journal of Human Resources* 14.1: 3-20.

Cotton, Jeremiah. 1988. "On the Decomposition of Wage Differentials." *Review of Economics and Statistics* 70.2: 236–243.

Darity, William A., Jr. 1980. "Illusions of Black Economic Progress." *Review of Black Political Economy* 10.2: 151–168.

Darity, William A. And Samuel L. Myers. 1993. "Racial Earnings Inequality and Family Structure." Mimeograph. University of Minnesota.

Doeringer, Peter B. And Michael J. Piore. 1971. *Internal Labor Markets and Manpower Analysis.* Lexington, Mass: D.C. Heath.

Duncan, Greg J. And Saul D. Hoffman. 1983. "A New Look at the Causes of the Improved Economic Status of Black Workers." *Journal of Human Resources* 17.2: 268–282.

Duncan, Otis Dudley and Beverly Duncan. 1955. "A Methodological Analysis of Segregation Indexes." *American Sociological Review* 20: 210–217.

Edgeworth, F.J. 1922. "Equal Pay to Men and Women for Equal Work." *Economic Journal* 32: 431–457.

Ehrenberg, Ronald G. and Robert S. Smith. 1944. *Modern Labor Economics.* 5th edition. Glenview, Ill: Scott Foresman.

England, Paula. 1981. "Assessing Trends in Occupational Sex Segregation, 1900–1976," *Sociological Perspectives on Labor Markets.* Ed. Ivar Berg. New York: Academic Press. 273–296.

England, Paula. 1982. "The Failure of Human Capital Theory to Explain Occupational Sex Segregation." *Journal of Human Resources* 17.3: 358–370.

Ferguson, D.C. 1969. *Microeconomic Theory.* Revised ed. Homewood, Ill: Richard Irwin, 1969.

Filer, Randall K. 1985. "Male-Female Wage Differences: The Importance of Compensating Differentials." *Industrial and Labor Relations Review* 38.3: 426–437.

Franklin, R.J. and S. Resnik. 1974. *The Political Economy of Racism.* New York: Holt, Rinehart, Winston.

Freeman, Richard B. 1973. "Changes in the Labor Market for Black Americans, 1948–1972. *Brookings Progress on Economic Activity I.*

Freeman, Richard B. 1981. "Have Black Labor Market Gains Been Permanent or Transitory?" Harvard Institute of Economic Research, Discussion Paper No. 849.

Freeman, Richard B. and James L. Medoff. 1979. "New Estimates of Private Sector Unionism in the United States." *Industrial and Labor Relations Review* 32.2: 143–174.

Friedman, Milton. 1962. *Capitalism and Freedom.* Chicago: University of Chicago Press.

Friedman, Samuel. 1984. "Structure, Process, and the Labor Market." *Labor Economics: Modern Views.* Ed. William Darity, Jr. Boston: Kluwer-Nijhoff Publishing. 53–89.

Fujii, Edwin T. And James Mak. 1983b. "The Determinants of Income of Native- and Foreign-born Men in a Multiracial Society." *Applied Economics* 15: 759–776.

Gabriel, Paul E., Donald R. Williams, Susanne Schmitz. 1990. The Relative Occupational Attainment of Young Blacks, Whites, and Hispanics." *Southern Economic Journal* 57: 35–46.

Gaston, Robert J. 1972. "Labor Market Conditions and Employer Hirisng Standards." *industrial Relations* 11.2: 1972.

Gilroy, Curtis L. 1975. "Investment in Human Capital and Blac-White Unemployment." *Monthly Labor Review* 98.5: 13–21.

Goodman, J.F.B. 1970. "The Definition and Analysis of Local Labour Markets: Some Empirical Problems." *British Journal of Industrial Relations* 8: 179–196.

Goldberg, Matthew S. 1982. "Discrimination, Neoptism, and Long-Run Wage Differentials." *The Quarterly Journal of Economics.* 97.2: 307–319.

Goldner, William. 1955. "Spatial and Locational Aspects of Metropolitan Labor Markets." *American Economic Review* 45: 113–128.

Gunderson, Morley. 1989. "Male-Female Wage Differentials and Policy Responses." *Journal of Economic Literature.* 27: 46–72.

Gwartney, James D. And James E. Long. 1978. "The Relative Earnings of Blacks and Other Minorities." *Industrial and Labor Relations Review* 31: 336–346.

Gwartney, James D. And R. Stroup. 1973. "Measurement of Employment Discrimination According to Sex." *Southern Economic Journal* 39: 575–587.

Hanoch, Giora. 1967. "An Economic Analysis of Earnings and Schooling." *Journal of Human Resources* 2: 310–329.

Hanushek, Eric A. 1981. "Alternative Models of Earnings Determination and Labor Market Structures." *Journal of Human Resources* 16: 239-259.

Hanushek, Eric A. 1973. "Regional Differences in The Structure of Earnings." *Review of Economics and Statistics* 55.2: 204–213.

Heckman, James J. 1980. "Sample Selection Bias as a Specification Error." In James P. Smith, ed., *Female Labor Supply: Theory and Estimation.* Princeton, N.J.: Princeton University Press. 206–248.

Heckman, James J. and Brook S. Payner. 1989. "Determining the Impact of Federal Antidiscrimination Policy on the Economic Status of Blacks: A Study of South Carolina." *American Economic Review.* 79.1: 138–177.

Heckman, James J. And Solomon Polachek. 1974. "Empirical Evidence on the Functional Form of the Earnings — Schooling Relationship." *Journal of the American Statistical Association* 69: 35–54.

Hendricks, Wallace. 1977. "Regulation and Labor Earnings." *The Bell Journal of Economics.* 8.2:483–496.

Hirsch, Barry T. 1978. "Predicting Earnings Distributions Across Cities: The Human Capital Model vs. The National Distribution Hypothesis." *Journal of Human Resources* 13: 366–384.

Hirsch, Barry T. and John T. Addison. 1986. *The Economic Analysis of Uniions.* Boston: Allen and Unwin.

Hsaio, Cheng. 1986. *Analysis of Panel Data.* Cambridge: Cambridge University Press.

Hyclak, Thomas and Geriant Johnes. 1987. "One the Determinants of Full Employment Unemployment Rates in Local Labour Markets." *Applied Economics* 19: 191–200.

Hyclak, Thomas. 1979. "The Effect of Unions on Earnings Inequality in Local Labor Markets." *Industrial and Labor Relations Review* 33.1: 77-84.

Iden, George. 1967. "Unemployment Classification of Major Labor Areas, 1950–65." *Journal of Human Resources* 2.3: 375–391.

Johnson, William. 1978. "Racial Wage Discrimination and Industrial Structure." *The Bell Journal of Economics.* 9.1: 70–81.

Johnston, John. 1984. *Econometric Methods*. New York: McGraw Hill.

Joll, Caroline, Chris McKenna, Robert McNabb, and John Shorey. 1983. *Developments in Labour Market Analysis*. London: George Allen and Unwin.

Jones, F.L. 1983. "On Decomposing the Wage Gap: A Critical Comment on Blinder's Method." *Journal of Human Resources* 18: 126–130.

Kiefer, Nicholas M. And Sharon Smith. 1977. "Union Impact and Wage Discrimination by Region." *Journal of Human Resources* 12.4: 521–534.

King, Mary C. 1992. "Occupational Segregation by Race and Sex, 1940–88." *Monthly Labor Review* 115.4: 30-37.

Kokkelenberg, Edward and Donna Sockell. 1985. "Union Membership in the United States, 1973–1981." *Industrial and Labor Relations Review* 38.4: 497–543.

Krueger, Anne O. 1963. "The Economics of Discrimination." *Journal of Political Economy* 71: 481–486.

Leonard, Jonathan S. 1984a. "Employment and Occupational Advance Under Affirmative Action." *The Review of Economics and Statistics*. 66.3: 377–385.

Loenard, Jonathan S. 1984b. "The Impact of Affirmative Action on Employment." *Journal of Labor Economics*. 2.4: 439–463.

Lloyd, Cynthia B. And Beth T. Niemi. 1979. *The Economics of Sex Differentials*. New York: Columbia University Press.

Long, James and Albert Link. 1983. "The Impact of Market Structure on Wages, Fringe Benefits, and Turnover." *Industrial and Labor Relations Review*. 36.2: 239–250.

Lydall, Harold. 1968. *The Structure of Earnings*. Oxford: Clarendon Pres.

Lyson, Thomas A. 1985. "Race and Sex Segregation in the Occupational Structures of Southern Employrs." *Social Science Quarterly* 66.2: 281–295.

Madden, Janice Fanning. 1975. "Discrimination — A Manifestation of Market Power?" *Sex, Discrimination, and the Division of Labor.* Ed. Cynthia B. Lloyd. New York: Columbia University Press. 146–174.

Madden, Janice Fanning. 1973. *The Economics of Sex Discrimination.* Lexington, Mass.: D.C. Heath and Company.

Marshall, Ray. 1974. "The Economics of Racial Discrimination: A Survey." *Journal of Economic Literature* 12: 849–871.

McConnell, Campbell and Stanley Brue. 1995. *Contemporary Labor Economics.* 4th ed. New York: McGraw Hill.

McCrackin, Bobbie. 1984. "Education's Contribution to Productivity and Economic Growth." *Economic Review: Federal Reserve Bank of Atlanta* 69.10: 8–23.

Miller, Paul W. and Paul A. Volker. 1985. "On the Determination of Occupational Attainment and Mobility." *Journal of Human Resources* 20: 197–213.

Mincer, Jacob. 1970. "The Distribution of Labor Incomes: A Survey." *Journal of Economic Literature* 8: 1–26.

Mincer, Jacob. 1974. *Schooling, Experience, and Earnings.* New York: National Bureau of Economic Research.

Mincer, Jacob and Solomon Polachek. 1974. "Family Investments in Human Capital: Earnings of Women." *Journal of Political Economy* 82: S76–S108.

Murphy, Kevin J. 1985. "Geographic Differences in U.S. Unemployment Rates: A Variance Decomposition Approach." *Economic Inquiry* 23: 135–158.

Murphy, Kevin and Richard Hofler. 1984. "Determinants of Geographic Unemployment Rates: A Selectively Pooled-Simultaneous Model." *Review of Economics and Statistics* 66: 216–223.

Murphy, Kevin and Finis Welch. 1987. "The Structure of Wages." University of Chicago.

Neumark, David. 1988. "Employer's Discriminatory Behavior and the Estimation of Wage Discrimination." *The Journal of Human Resources.* 23: 279–295.

Nord, Stephen. 1987. "Productivity and the Role of College in Narrowing the Male-Female Wage Differential in the U.S.A. in 1980." *Applied Economics* 19: 51–67.

Oaxaca, Ronald. 1973a. "Male-Female Differentials in Urban Labor Markets." *International Economic Review* 14: 693–709.

Oaxaca, Ronald. 1973b. "Sex Discrimination in Wages." *Discrimination in Labor Markets.* Eds. Orley Ashenfelter and A. Rees. Princeton: Princeton University Press. 124–151.

O'Neill, June. 1985. "The Trend in the Male-Female Wage Gap in the United States." *Journal of Labor Economics* 3: S91–S116.

O'Neill, June and Solomon Polachek. 1993. "Why the Gender Gap in Wages Narrowed in the 1980's?" *Journal of Labor Economics.* H.1: 205–228.

Piore, Michael (Ed.). 1979b. *Unemployment and Inflation: Institutionalist and Structuralist Views.* White Plains: M. Sharpe.

Polachek, Solomon William. 1981. "Occupational Self-Selection: A Human Capital Approach to Sex Differences in Occupational Structure." *Review of Economics and Statistics* 63: 60–69.

Reder, Melvin W. 1973. "Comment." *Discrimination in Labor Markets.* Ed. Orley Ashenfelter and Albert Rees. Princeton: Princeton University Press. 3–33.

Reich, Michael J. 1981. *Racial Inequality: A Political Economic Analysis*. Princeton: Princeton University Press.

Reich, Michael J., David M. Gordon, and Richard C. Edwards. 1973. "A Theory of Labor Market Segmentation." *American Economic Review* 63: 359–365.

Reimers, Cordelia W. 1983. "Labor Market Discrimination Against Hispanic and Black Men." *The Review of Economics and Statistics* 65.4: 570–579.

Rosen, Sherwin. 1972. "Learning and Experience in the Labor Market." *Journal of Human Resources* 7: 326–342.

Rosen, Sherwin. 1977. "Human Capital: A Survey of Empirical Research." *Research in Labor Economics* Ed. 3–39.

Rosenweig, Mark R. And Jack Morgan. 1976. "An Exchange: On the Appropriate Specification of Human Capital Models." *Journal of Human Resources* 11: 3–7.

Saaxonhouse, Gary R. 1976. "Estimated Parameters as Dependent Variables." *American Economic Review* 66:178–183.

Saunders, Lisa. 1995. "Relative Earnings of Black Men to White Men by Region, Industry." *Monthly Labor Review* 118.4: 68–73.

Schultze, Theodore W. 1961. "Investments in Human Capital." *American Economic Review* 51: 1–17.

Shackett, Joyce R. and John M. Trapani. 1987. "Earnings Differential and Market Structure." *Journal of Human Resources* 22.4: 518–531.

Shulman, Steven. 1987. "Discrimination, Human Capital, and Black-White Unemployment: Evidence from Cities." *Journal of Human Resources* 22.3: 361–376.

Shulman, Steven. 1984a. "Competition and Racial Discrimination: The Employment Effects of Reagan's Labor Market Policies." *Review of Radical Political Economics* 16.4: 111–128.

Shulman, Steven. 1984b. "Black Wage and Occupational Gains: A Reevaluation." *Review of Black Political Economy* 12: 59–69.

Siegel, Sidney and John Castellan, Jr. 1988. *Nonparametric Statistics for the Behavioral Sciences.* New York: McGraw Hill.

Smith, James. 1984. "Race and Human Capital." *American Economic Review* 74: 685–698.

Smith, James P.and Finis R. Welch. 1989. "Black Economic Progress After Myrdal." *Journal of Economic Literature.* 27.2: 519–564.

Smith, James P. and Finis R.Welch. 1977. "Black-White Male Wage Ratios: 1960–1970." *American Economic Review* 67: 323–338.

Smith, Sharon P. 1976. "Government Wage Differentials by Sex." *Journal of Human Resources* 11: 185–199.

Stiglitz, Joseph E. 1973. "Pproaches to the Economics of Discrimination." *American Economic Review* 63: 287–295.

Tobin, James. 1965. "On Improving the Economic Status of the Negro." *Daedalus.* 94: 878–898.

Topel, Robert H. 1984. "Equilibrium Earnings, Turnover and Unemployment: New Evidence." *Journal of Labor Economics* 2.4: 500–522.

Topel, Robert H. 1986. "Local Labor Markets." *Journal of Political Economy* 94.3 Part2: S111–S143.

Twomey, David P. 1990. *Equal Employment Opportunity Law.* 3rd Edition. Cincinnati: South-Western.

U.S. Council of Economic Advisors. 1980. *Economic Report of the President.* Washington: G.P.O.

U.S. Department of Commerce. Bureau of the Census. 1973a. *1970 Census of Population: Vol. 1, Characteristics of the Population, General*

Social and Economic Characteristics. United States Summary. Washington: G.P.O.

U.S. Department of Commerce. Bureau of the Census. 1973b. *County and City Data Book 1972 (A Statistical Abstract Supplement).* Washington: G.P.O.

U.S. Department of Commerce. Bureau of the Census. 1977. *Public Use Samples of Basic Records from the 1970 Census: Description and Technical Documentation.* Washington: G.P.O.

U.S. Department of Commerce. Bureau of the Census. 1982a. *1980 Census of Population and Housing User's Guide Part A Text.* Washington: G.P.O.

U.S. Department of Commerce. Bureau of the Census. 1982b. *State and Metropolitan Area Data Book 1982 (A Statistical Abstract Supplement).* Washington: G.P.O.

U.S. Department of Commerce. Bureau of the Census. 1983a. *1980 Census of Population: Vol. 1, Characteristics of the Population, General Social and Economic Characteristics. United States Summary.* Washington: G.P.O.

U.S. Department of Commerce. Bureau of the Census. 1983b. *Census of the Population and Housing: 1980 Technical Documentation.* Washington: G.P.O

U.S. Department of Commerce. Bureau of the Census. 1984a. *1980 Census of Population: Vol. 1, Characteristics of the Population, Detailed Population Characteristics. United States Summary.* Washington: G.P.O.

U.S. Department of Commerce. Bureau of the Census. 1984b. *1980 Census of Population: Vol. 2, Subject Reports, Geographical Mobility for Metropolitan Areas.* Washington: G.P.O.

United States Department of Labor. Bureau of Labor Statistics. *Employment and Earnings* 29: 157-160. January 1981.

U.S. Equal Employment Opportunity Commission. 1981. *Laws Administered by EEOC*. Washington: G.P.O.

Watts, Martin. 1995. "Divergent Trends in Gender Segregation by Occupation in the United States: 1970-92." *Journal of Post Keynesian Economics* 17: 357-379.

Watts, Martin. 1992. "How Should Occupational Sex Segregation Be Measured?" *Work, Employment and Society* 6: 475-487.

Westcott, Diane N. 1982. "Blacks in the 1970's: Did They Scale the Job Ladder?" *Monthly Labor Review* 105.6: 29-38.

Williams, Rhonda M. 1984. "The Methodology and Practice of Modern Labor Economics: A Critique." *Labor Economics: Modern Views*. Ed. William Darity, Jr. Boston: Kluwer-Nijhoff Publishing. 53-89.

Zellner, Harriet. 1972. "Discrimination Against Women, Occupational Segregation, and the Relative Wage." *American Economic Review* 62: 157-160.

Index

For Product Safety Concerns and Information please contact our EU representative GPSR@taylorandfrancis.com Taylor & Francis Verlag GmbH, Kaufingerstraße 24, 80331 München, Germany

Printed and bound by CPI Group (UK) Ltd, Croydon, CR0 4YY

08/05/2025

01864447-0001